Charles Dexter Cleveland, Salmon P. (Salmon Portland) Chase, (Pa.)
Liberty Party

Anti-slavery addresses of 1844 and 1845

Charles Dexter Cleveland, Salmon P. (Salmon Portland) Chase, (Pa.) Liberty Party

Anti-slavery addresses of 1844 and 1845

ISBN/EAN: 9783744737968

Printed in Europe, USA, Canada, Australia, Japan

Cover: Foto ©ninafisch / pixelio.de

More available books at **www.hansebooks.com**

ANTI-SLAVERY ADDRESSES

OF

1844 AND 1845.

BY

SALMON PORTLAND CHASE

AND

CHARLES DEXTER CLEVELAND.

LONDON:

SAMPSON LOW, SON, AND MARSTON,

MILTON HOUSE, LUDGATE HILL.

PHILADELPHIA: J. A. BANCROFT AND CO.

1867.

PHILADELPHIA ADDRESS.

PREFACE.

HE great contest in our country between Freedom and Slavery began with the very formation of our Constitution, and continued, with various intermissions, down to the overthrow of the giant-monster by the proclamation of our martyr-President—Abraham Lincoln—January 1, 1863. As the future historian will desire as many landmarks as possible of this great life-and-death struggle, the following Addresses are now re-published in a form more permanent than when they first appeared. It is now nearly a quarter of a century since they were written. A new generation has come upon the stage, comparatively ignorant of the opposition encountered and the odium endured by those who thus early fought the great battle of Freedom. We fought, indeed, with the moral weapons of justice, conscience, and the Word of God; but urged, at the same time, that all these should be consummated at the ballot-box. We hoped and prayed for the peaceful overthrow of slavery by legislative enactments, and we asked all classes to aid us. We asked "Whigs" to vote against the vilest oligarchy that the sun ever shone upon, and in accordance with those true principles of Freedom with which their name had

been for centuries so honourably associated. We asked
" Democrats " to bear in mind the true meaning of the
word they had so constantly in their mouths ; and so to
vote as to secure the ascendancy of *true* Democracy
everywhere—the rights of man *as man*, without distinction of colour, country, or condition. And we asked
Christians simply to vote as they prayed. But no : the
" Whigs " seemed to care more for " national banks,"
and " tariffs," and " internal improvements," than the
eternal principles of justice, and the inalienable rights
of man. The " Democrats" seemed to think more how
they should so " join hand in hand" with their " Southern
brethren " as to secure to themselves the spoils of office.
And the Christian, while he would pray at the evening
prayer-meeting that our country might be governed by
" righteous men ruling in the fear of God," would vote
the next day for those who seemed to say in their hearts
—" How doth God know ; and is there knowledge in
the Most High ? " Alas ! He has since shown us *how*
He " knew," in the terrible judgments with which He
has visited us for our great national sin.

Despairing, therefore, of winning over either of the
two great parties to the cause of Freedom, the ardent
friends of Liberty determined to organize a new party
founded on its sacred principles. The consciences as
well as the indignation of a large number in the Free
States had been aroused by the triumphs of the slave
power in the long-contested Missouri struggle in 1820
and 1821 ; and in 1836 some earnest abolitionists in
New York nominated and voted for an anti-slavery
candidate for the Presidency, though there was no
national organization. By the time, however, that the

next presidential election came around in 1840, the "National Liberty Party" was organized, and James G. Binney, its candidate for the Presidency, received seven thousand votes. At the next election, in 1844, he received nearly seventy thousand; and in 1848 Martin Van Buren, the "free-soil" candidate, received about two hundred and fifty thousand. Thus the party for Freedom, so small and so despised at first, grew stronger and stronger every year, until in 1860 it placed Abraham Lincoln in the presidential chair. Then, as is well known, the slave-power, despairing of any longer controlling the counsels of the government, as it had done for half a century, raised the standard of rebellion to overthrow that government, and that, too, to found another "whose corner-stone should be Slavery." But, blessed be God, that, though encouraged and aided by too many traitors in the North, they were utterly thwarted in their infernal purpose, and that no portion of our country is now, or ever again can be, trodden by the foot of a slave.

It is to be hoped that in the earlier days of this long contest between Freedom and Slavery, the following Addresses exerted their share of influence for the righteous cause, and in ultimately bringing about the auspicious result—of Freedom's being inaugurated in our public counsels. But, however this may be, the authors are more than willing to present them now to the present generation and for future times exactly as they were then written, and thus to contribute another mite to the permanent anti-slavery literature of their country.   C. D. C.

London, May, 1867.

NOTE.

OF the two Addresses I place the Philadelphia first, simply because it was the first in the order of time. Had I placed them according to their merits, the Cincinnati Address would, of course, come first; and the other next indeed, but, in the expressive language of Milton—"long after next."

C. D. C.

ADDRESS OF THE

LIBERTY PARTY OF PENNSYLVANIA

TO THE PEOPLE OF THE

STATE.*

FRIENDS AND FELLOW CITIZENS.

A T a Convention of Delegates of the Liberty Party of the Eastern section of Pennsylvania, held in Philadelphia, Feb. 22, 1844, the undersigned was made the chairman of a committee appointed to address you upon the great cause which we are laboring to promote. We now, therefore, proceed to set before you our views, our principles, and our aims; to state the means by which we believe those aims will be ac-

---

* I may now (1867) here state these facts, that the Liberty Committee ordered, at first, twenty thousand copies of this address to be printed, and the types to be kept standing, as it was not stereotyped; and that two editions more, of twenty thousand each, were subsequently printed.

complished ; and to invite your cordial and earnest co-operation with us, to secure such results as, we are sure, will be for the best good both of our State and of our country.

PRINCIPLES OF THE PARTY.

In the first place, then, we would state, that the Liberty Party, though new in its organization, is not new in its principles. It is, in the great elements of its character, only an old party revived. It is, in its principles, the same party as that which, in 1776, rallied around the Declaration of Independence, and " pledged their lives, their fortunes, and their sacred honor," to maintain the noble sentiments avowed in that instrument, that " all men are created equal, and are endowed by their Creator with the unalienable rights of life, liberty, and the pursuit of happiness." It is, in its principles, the same party as that which, in 1787, formed our own federal Constitution, the great object of which, as set forth in the preamble, is " to establish *justice*—to promote the *general welfare*—and to secure the *blessings of liberty*." It is, in its principles, the same party that, in the same year, in the Congress of the old Confederation, passed, unanimously, that ever-to-be-honoured Ordinance, in which it is declared that the whole territory of our country North and West of the river Ohio, should never be trodden by the foot of a slave.

Such, fellow citizens, are the principles of our party. We cherish the same views as Washington, who wrote these very words,—" There is but one effectual mode by which the abolition of slavery can be accomplished, and that is *by legislative authority,* and this, so far as my SUFFRAGE will go, SHALL NOT BE WANTING." We cherish the same views as Patrick Henry, who declared " that we owe it to the purity of our religion, to show that it is at variance with that law which warrants slavery."* We cherish the same views as Robert Morris, who, in the Convention for forming the Constitution, pronounced slavery to be "a nefarious institution." We cherish the same views as William Pinckney, who said in the House of Delegates of Maryland, in 1789, " By the eternal principles of natural justice, no master in this state has a right to hold his slave for a single hour." We cherish the same views as Jefferson, who uttered these memorable words, " I tremble for my country when I reflect that God is just, and that his justice cannot sleep forever." We cherish

---

* In a letter dated January 18, 1773, Patrick Henry thus wrote :—" Is it not a little surprising that the professors of Christianity, whose chief excellence consists in softening the human heart, and in cherishing and improving its finer feelings, should encourage a practice so totally repugnant to the first principles of right and wrong ?" Again he says :— " It would rejoice my very soul that every one of my fellow beings was emancipated. Believe me, I shall ever honour the Quakers for their noble efforts to abolish slavery."

the same views as Dr. Rush, who declared slavery to be " repugnant to the principles of Christianity, and rebellion against the authority of a common Father." And we cherish the same views as Madison, who said, in the Convention of 1787, that it was " wrong to admit into the Constitution even the idea that there could be property in man."

Yes, fellow citizens, these men of former days, and many more that might be named, saw and felt the evils of slavery. They saw that it must be a curse to any country; and they saw the great inconsistency of cherishing it in our own. They saw, too, that if they themselves had any right, in 1776, to resist unto blood for a pound of tea, the slave had an infinitely higher right to make the same resistance for an infinitely higher object. This, one of these patriot spirits had the candour to express, declaring " that in such a contest the Almighty had no attributes which could take sides with the master." The men of those days looked forward, confidently, to the speedy extinction of slavery. In the Conventions of several of the States that met to ratify the Constitution, these opinions were unequivocally expressed. In the Convention of Massachusetts Judge Dawes remarked, that " slavery had received its death-wound, and would die of consumption." In the Convention of Pennsylvania, Judge Wilson, himself one of the framers of the Constitution, said, " The new States which are to be formed will be under the control of Congress, in this particular, AND SLAVERY WILL NEVER BE INTRODUCED AMONG THEM." And that great man, whose illustrious example can never be too often held up to us for imitation—General Washington—wrote to John Sinclair, " The abolition of slavery must take place, and that too at a period NOT REMOTE."

Such, fellow citizens, were the opinions of the men who laid the foundations of our republic; men of high, noble, wide-reaching views; and who feared that nothing would so endanger the permanency of the fair fabric which their wisdom had reared, as the continuation of slavery. Far different, indeed, felt and spoke and wrote those men, from many of our modern, so-called statesmen: far different from the Calhouns and the McDuffies, who declare " slavery to be the corner-stone of our republican institutions :" far different from Henry Clay, who has proclaimed, unblushingly, that he is opposed to " any emancipation, immediate or gradual ;" and who pronounced the opinion of Madison, " that man cannot hold property in man," to be a " visionary dogma :" far different from Martin Van Buren, who pledged himself before election to veto any bill that Congress might pass to abolish slavery in the District of Columbia : and far different from many other prominent men of our times, whose highest ambition, we feel constrained to say, seems to be, to cringe to the slave power.

We will now, therefore, proceed to set before you, historically, and in a very succinct manner, these

CHANGES AND THEIR CAUSES.

VERY soon after the formation of our Constitution, the slaveholders saw the great political power which, for the sake of peace and union, its framers had given them ; and they determined to use it for their own aggrandizement. Whether there was any express understanding, or any secret compact among them, that in all questions touching slavery they would go together as one man, can never be known. Be this, however, as it may, the fact that they have done so remains, and it is clear to every one who knows anything of the history of our country. No matter what other questions, apparently of momentous interest, have distracted different parties; here the slaveholders, true to their instincts, have presented but one undivided front.

DISTRICT OF COLUMBIA.

IN the year 1790, Congress accepted from the States of Maryland and Virginia the territory of ten miles square, now the District of Columbia, for the purpose of locating there the capitol of the nation. When these states ceded this territory to Congress, they " relinquished the same to the government of the United States, in full and absolute right and

exclusive jurisdiction,"* and all the state laws that
before had existence there, became, of course, by that
very act, null and void. The very act of Congress in that year, in relation to this subject, shows
this truth most conclusively; for that act ordained
that the laws of Maryland and Virginia should continue in force until otherwise ordered. To pass an
act for their continuance is, of course, a full admission that they would not continue without such an
act. That act, therefore, is precisely the same as if
Congress had enacted an entire new code for the per-
petuity of slavery there. Had it any right to do this
CONSTITUTIONALLY? Clearly not. To argue that
it had, would be to argue against the sun. The constitution gives no power to Congress to establish
slavery. The men who framed that instrument
would not allow the word "slave" to be inserted in
it. Its preamble declares one of its objects to be to
"secure the blessings of liberty," not the curse of
slavery; and article fifth of the Amendments reads
thus: "No person shall be deprived of *liberty* without due process of law." The act of Congress,
therefore, that was framed to introduce slavery into
the District of Columbia, was a plain, open, total
violation of the constitution. But the Slave power
went unitedly for it, and the deed was done. But
every man, woman, and child, there held as a slave,

---

* See Act of the State of Maryland, passed December 19,
1791.

is at this moment virtually free; and the Supreme
Court of the United States would doubtless so decide, were it not for the fact, to which we shall
soon particularly allude, that a majority of its judges
are from the Slave states.

And now we ask you, fellow citizens, to look at
this subject for one moment longer. Look at the
capitol of our nation, over which Congress, in the
words of the Constitution, "exercises exclusive legislation in all cases whatever;" look at it, transformed
into a slave-market, the most extensive and loath-
some of any in the world. See there, the domestic
slave trade vigorously and unblushingly carried on
in open day, a trade, which Judge Cranch and
eleven hundred other citizens of the District, in a
memorial to Congress in 1828, declare to be "more
cruel in its operations and more demoralizing in its
effects than the African slave trade itself." See
there, in the daily papers, standing advertisements
for the purchase of men, women, and children. See
there, every two or three weeks, cargoes of human
beings shipped on board vessels for a Southern
market, like so many beasts. Like beasts, did we
say? Aye, worse; for, horrid as it is, *they are*
FETTERED, TWO AND TWO, IN IRONS; and should
any accident happen to the vessel, they have not
even the chance of making an exertion for their
safety; but, as in that awful case that lately occurred near the mouth of the Ohio, may see others
saving themselves, while they, helpless and un-

pitied, must go at once, with their heavy irons fastened about them, deep, deep to the bottom.

And how, fellow citizens, think you, these slaves are kept in security, until they can be safely shipped? We will tell you. To a considerable extent in jails, built by your money, supported by your money, protected by your money. These, with the private prisons, are the receptacles for the safe keeping of husbands separated from wives, and wives separated from husbands; of children from parents, and parents from children; until, as they term it, "a cargo can be made up." Men of Pennsylvania! ye who enjoy the blessings of freedom unmolested; ye who can look around on the happy faces at your own fireside, and feel that, in subjection only to the Providence of God, they are all your own, and that no spoiler's hand can snatch one of that endeared group away, will you not feel in a case like this? Aye, and will you not act, too? How? you may say. How? By giving your vote for such men to fill all our public offices, from the highest to the lowest, as will exert all the power they can, to put an end to this abomination; to this deep, foul, national disgrace. If the Slave states, in order to prop up a little longer their heaven-daring system, will send men to Congress to legislate FOR Slavery, will not you have the humanity as well as the manliness, to send men who will legislate AGAINST it?

But we cannot enlarge upon this subject, full of

interest though it be, but will next, in historical
order advert to

THE PURCHASE OF LOUISIANA IN 1803.

FIFTEEN millions of dollars of the people's money
were paid to France for this territory, and when the
purchase was made, French law, which before had
obtained there, ceased, and it was the duty of Congress to adopt the same measures in relation to this
territory, as it adopted in 1787 in relation to the
North West Territory, namely, TO MAKE IT FREE.
But no, this would not suit the slaveholders, and it
was not done; and thenceforth that vast territory
was to have its rich soil moistened with the tears and
blood of the slave.   The consequences are already
seen. Three states have already been formed out of it,
having now ten votes in the House of Representatives, and six votes, *almost one-eighth*, in the Senate
of the United States.   Here you see another of the
monstrous encroachments of the Slave power upon
constitutional liberty.   Next in order, we will in-
introduce you to

THE PURCHASE OF FLORIDA IN 1821.

THIS was purchased of Spain; and again it became
the duty of Congress to make such provisions, that
a slave should never tread its soil. Slavery, we know,
is not a state of nature, and the right to hold a slave

is not a natural, but a legal right. Slavery is a creature of positive law, and exists within those limits, and within those limits ONLY, where the laws that sanction it have force. The second clause of section second, article fourth, of the Constitution, says, "Congress shall have power to make all needful rules and regulations respecting the territories belonging to the United States;" and article fifth of the "Amendments," reads, "No person shall be deprived of *liberty* without due process of law:" while the preamble declares one of its objects to be, "to secure the blessings of *liberty.*"

Now, what are the facts? We all know them, and know them too well. There are now, according to the last census, in the territory of Florida, twenty-five thousand seven hundred and seventeen human beings held in slavery there, in utter, shameless defiance of the Constitution. And what have been the consequences to this nation? Since 1836, more than FORTY MILLIONS of dollars have been expended on the Florida war, for the special benefit of the slaveholder, to drive the red man from his native forests and from the graves of his fathers, that he might not be able to give shelter to those who should fly to him for protection from the hand of oppression and tyranny. We first purchase Florida for FIVE MILLIONS, and then expend FORTY MILLIONS MORE, that the slaveholder may hold his victims with a more secure grasp. But the money, enormous as is the amount, and coming home as it does to every man in the country, is nothing, and less than nothing, when we look at the lives sacrificed, the miseries endured, the cruelties practised, and every principle of honor and justice and humanity outraged and trampled on. Men of Pennsylvania! have you not SOMETHING to do with slavery?

MISSOURI STRUGGLE IN 1820-22.

THE next instance of the alarming extension of the Slave power, and one ever to be remembered, was the admission of Missouri into the Union as a slave state. In 1820, the "District of Maine" petitioned for admission into the Union. It was proper that she should be admitted; she had all the requisite qualifications, and no objections could be made to her on independent grounds. But the Slave power, with HENRY CLAY, then Speaker of the House, at their head, declared, unequivocally, their firm and determined hostility to the admission of Maine, until Missouri should have been admitted as a Slave state. The struggle was long and severe. The debate on the subject was protracted through two sessions, and the excitement throughout the country was intense. The representatives from the Free states showed more spirit, more manliness, and a firmer determination to defend the Constitution from violation than they have ever done since; and one of our own representatives, John

Sergeant, delivered, on that occasion, a speech to which Pennsylvanians will ever be proud to refer. At first, the friends of freedom were in a majority. But the slaveholders, never for a moment relaxing in their vigilance, continued to move on in solid column; and soon gained over enough of Northern votes to turn the scale, and thus that execrable project was finally carried, in utter defiance of every principle of natural justice, and of the letter, as well as of the general spirit of the Constitution.

Lastly, but six months ago, a most nefarious plot was matured by the President and the Southern members of his cabinet, in a manner as mean from its secrecy, as the measure itself was daring in its wickedness—A PLOT TO ANNEX TEXAS TO THE UNITED STATES.

Such is one class of facts, in the history of our country, to show the alarmingly increasing influence of the Slave power in the councils of the nation. Let us now proceed to another class of facts.

PREPONDERANCE OF THE SLAVE POWER IN ALL THE MOST IMPORTANT OFFICES OF GOVERNMENT.

1. *Presidents.*

SINCE the organization of our government, the Slaveholding states have had six Presidents, who will have served, at the end of this term, FORTY-

THREE YEARS AND ELEVEN MONTHS; the Free states, FOUR, who have served TWELVE YEARS AND ONE MONTH : and one of these four, Martin Van Buren, was elected on the ground of his being "a Northern man with Southern principles." And be it remembered, that no President from the Free states has ever been elected for a second term.

2. *Secretaries of State.*

Next in importance to the President is the office of Secretary of State. He it is that has the management of all the business and correspondence with foreign courts; that instructs all ambassadors, ministers, commissioners, and consuls; and that negotiates all the treaties. Of the sixteen Secretaries of State since the formation of the Constitution, the Slave states have had TWELVE, the Free states FOUR.

3. *The Judiciary.*

In the Judiciary, the very balance wheel of our government, and which has continually before it the most important questions of which man can take cognizance; questions of constitutional law; questions of chartered rights and privileges; questions involving millions of property; and above all, questions that are to decide the LIBERTY OR SLAVERY OF MAN; here, we say, the preponderance of the Slave power is still more alarming.

First, look at the Districts, and see how unequally, how unjustly they are divided. Vermont,

Connecticut, and New York constitute one District, with one Judge. They have forty-two Representatives in Congress, and a free population of 3,030,826; while Alabama and Louisiana, with but eleven Representatives, and with a free population of but 521,183, a little more than ONE SIXTH of the former, constitute another District, with another Judge. Then compare, where the comparison comes more home to ourselves. New Jersey and Pennsylvania constitute the third District; Mississippi and Arkansas the ninth. The former has TWENTY-NINE Representatives in Congress, and a free population of 2,096,601; the latter, but FIVE Representatives in Congress, and but 258,079 of free population.

Second, look at the manner in which the bench of the Supreme Court of the United States has ever been, and still is constituted. Of the twenty-seven Judges of that Court, since the adoption of the Constitution, the Slave states have had SEVENTEEN, the Free states but TEN : and of the eighteen Attorneys-General, the number has been against us in the still greater ratio of THIRTEEN to FIVE. Within the last nine years, six appointments have been made to the bench of the Supreme Court, and *all these from the Slave states;* and that, too. men of Pennsylvania, when we had within our own domain such men as Binney, and Dallas, and Chauncey, and Sergeant, and Rogers, and Gibson ; men whom we know to be equal to any, and supe-

rior to most of those who now occupy the seats of
that high tribunal. Is there not something deep,
dark, designing in all this? Does not the Slave
power mean to keep, if it can, a majority of the
Judges on *their* side, to decide *their* way in all
questions involving human liberty? Who, with
his eyes open, can for one moment doubt it?

4. *Speakers of the House.*

But the Slave power is not content with all this.
It is determined, if it can, to give its own com-
plexion to our national legislation. To this end, it
has so managed, generally, that the Speaker of the
House of Representatives shall be identified with
its interests. He it is that appoints all the Committees of the House. These Committees report
on the various subjects committed to their charge,
and their reports are printed in large numbers, and
sent abroad on the wings of the wind, all over the
land. Look back, then, into the history of our
national legislation, and you will find that in thirty
elections for Speaker of the House of Representatives, the Slave states have secured their man
TWENTY-ONE times, or for *forty* years; the Free
states, NINE times, or for SEVENTEEN years.
With the exception of Mr. Taylor, of New York,
who served three years, THE FREE STATES HAVE
NOT GIVEN A SPEAKER TO THE HOUSE SINCE
1809. Then go over to the other side of the Capitol,
and you will find that of the seventy-six Presidents

of the Senate, *pro tempore*, the Slave states have had SIXTY, the Free states SIXTEEN.

But we have neither space nor time, fellow citizens, to take up all the Offices and Departments of our Government, and to comment upon each separately. We will therefore select a few, and place them in a tabular form, comparing the number of those furnished by the Free states with those furnished by the Slave states, and leave you to make your own comments.

	Free states.	Slave states.
Presidents	4	6
Secretaries of State . .	4	12
Judges of the Supreme Court .	10	17
Speakers of the House . .	9	21
Presidents of the Senate (*pro tem.*)	16	60
Attorneys-General . . .	5	13
Secretaries of War . . .	10	7
,, ,, Navy . . .	8	7
,, ,, Treasury . .	11	5
Postmasters-General . .	7	4
Ministers of all kinds to foreign powers	52	80
	136	232

We said that we would leave you to make your own comments. We cannot, however, but remark, that whenever Northern men have been elected or appointed to any of these high offices, Southern men, whose vigilance is worthy of a better cause, have always been very careful first to see that the persons thus selected have a " fellow feeling " with themselves on the subject of slavery.　In 1841, six persons, ALL FROM THE SLAVE STATES, had been nominated to diplomatic stations previous to the nomination of Edward Everett, of Massachusetts to the Court of St. James, and all were confirmed without hesitation ; but his nomination was laid on the table.　For what reason?　Because he was unfit for the station?　No! for no one doubted that in every intellectual qualification he was immeasurably superior to all the rest.　But—and mark it well, fellow citizens—because he was thought by the Southern senators not to favor sufficiently their *"peculiar institutions;"* a soft phrase which they use, we know, for *slavery*, when conscience, paying thus an involuntary tribute to justice and virtue, would cause the latter term to stick in their throat.　At the rejection of such a man, a few Northern editors did, for a time, shake off their mouse-like spirits, and speak out like men. The nomination was at last confirmed, but—and mark this, too—not until some of the Northern friends of Mr. Everett had the meanness so far to cringe to the Slave power, as to send letters to Washington to assure their " Southern friends " that he was not tinctured with " abolition senti-ments."　And within this year, of six nominations sent on one day to the Senate of the United States to fill important public stations, five were from the Northern and one from a Southern state; all from the Free states were rejected, while the one from Virginia was confirmed; though he had been a second in a duel, which, in a moment, made a wife a widow, and a family of children orphans.

THE SLAVE POWER CONTROLS THE GREAT INTERESTS OF OUR COUNTRY.

HAVING thus shown you, fellow citizens, the vast preponderance of the Slave power in all the important offices of our government, we will now proceed to set before you a few other facts, which prove, conclusively, how it has extended its power and exerted its influence in every possible direction, to the greatest injury of our country's best interests.

1. *The Navy.*

Ever since the glorious act of England in emancipating all the slaves in her West India colonies—an act which, from the most happy results that have followed, seems to be held up to the world as a signal example that it is always safe to do right, —the Slave power has been most vigilant in securing a preponderance in the Navy. The " Home Squadron " has been a favourite measure with them, that they might have protection for their infamous coastwise slave trade, as well as protection for their sea coast. A guilty conscience sees a thousand threatening dangers where an honest man sees none; and the slaveholder seems to have continually flitting before his distempered vision scores of vessels laden with armed free blacks from the West Indies, approaching our Southern shores, to avenge the cause of their brethren in bonds. Hence they have taken special care to have a majority of the officers of the Navy from their own states, and to have the Naval Bureaus at Washington under their own control.

Of the forty-three officers in the Navy Department in Washington, *thirty-one* are from the Slave states, and but *twelve* from the Free states ; and of all the officers in the Navy, whether in actual service or waiting orders, Pennsylvania, with a free population more than double that of Virginia, has but *one hundred and seventy-seven*, while Virginia has *two hundred and twenty-four*. The late Secretary of the Navy, Judge Upshur, in the first year of his office, appointed thirty-two midshipmen, of whom fifteen were taken from Virginia, and the other seventeen from Maryland, Delaware, and the District.—We might extend this train of remark to a great extent, but we have not space. The facts, however, show the deep, well-laid design of the Slave power to be, to secure the services of the Navy for the defence of Slavery, and, in the event of a war, to secure the possession of the Navy itself.

Look, now, fellow citizens, at the appropriations

for the fiscal year ending June, 1844. They are
—for the Army, more than two millions; for the
Fortifications, &c, more than four millions; for
the Navy, more than eight millions, and for the
Peace establishment, not quite seven millions of
dollars. Here, in a time of profound tranquillity,
the expenses for war are more than double those
for peace.

But why so much, you may ask, for the Navy?
We will tell you. The "Home Squadron" is to
consist, this year, of SIXTEEN vessels. Yes,
fellow citizens, to protect our own coasts, an establishment is to be kept up of three frigates, six
sloops, two steamers, and five brigs and schooners.
Do you ask the reason of all this array of
military force? Let the late Judge Upshur, the
Secretary of the Navy, himself from Virginia,
answer. In his late Report he speaks of "those
incursions from which so much evil is to be apprehended." Again: "The effect of these incursions,
on the Southern portion of our country, would be
disastrous in the extreme." And again: "The
Southern naval stations, MORE ESPECIALLY, require a large force for their security. A large
number of arms is kept in each of them, which, by
a sudden irruption of the class of PEOPLE *who are
not citizens*, might be seized and used for very
disastrous purposes."

Here, fellow citizens, you have the whole of it.
Here you see that we of the Free states are to be

taxed to an enormous amount, and that the power
of the General Government is to be used, to keep
the slaves of the Southern states from insurrection!
The question will not now, we think, be asked by
you—" What has the North to do with Slavery?"

2. *The Post Office.*

Scarcely any one of the great elements of modern
civilization is productive of more happy results to
a country than the post office system, when pro-
perly conducted; that system by which a Government takes upon itself the obligation to give to its
subjects or citizens the power of communicating
one with another, at any distance, throughout its
whole domain. But that this system may do the
most good, two things are essential; namely,
SECURITY and CHEAPNESS. The farmer, or the
merchant, or the tradesman, who wishes to learn
the state of the markets—the mechanic or laborer,
who desires to know the rate of wages—the friend,
who is anxious to hear of the welfare of a friend,
from whom he has long been parted—the mother or
the father, who wishes to hear from an absent child
—the emigrant, who has left the home of his youth,
and gone out into the far West, but who yet wishes
to gain frequent tidings from that spot he has left
behind, so dear to his memory;—all these should
be able to communicate with each other, *freely* and
safely, indeed, but CHEAPLY. THE GREATEST,
THE STRONGEST CEMENT OF OUR UNION, WOULD

BE A CHEAP RATE OF POSTAGE. In Great Britain, a Monarchy, a friend can send a letter to a friend to any part of the kingdom for TWO CENTS; while in republican America it would cost him, in most cases, from *six to twelve times that sum.*

Now, fellow citizens, let us tell you that *the great obstacle to a* SAFE *and* CHEAP *postage is the Slave power.* In 1835, Amos Kendall, the Postmaster General, to please the citizens of Charleston, South Carolina, wrote to the Postmaster there, "So far as I can prevent it no anti-slavery pamphlets or papers shall be circulated through the public mails;" and the citizens of that city met, and passed a series of resolutions, in which they declared themselves determined to resist, by FORCE, any attempt to send through the mail what they termed "incendiary pamphlets;" and actually opened a number of LETTERS, and *burnt a large number of papers and pamphlets!!* But this is not all. In the same year the Postmaster of New York "assumed the responsibility" of suppressing such papers as he thought proper, and of refusing the mail to such citizens as had sent to him some copies of the Anti-Slavery Reporter; and in the year 1838, a large number of the "Baltimore Religious Magazine," containing an article on "Bible Slavery," which did not please the slavebreeders of Petersburg, Virginia, were taken from the Post Office, and burnt

C

in the street, in *the presence, and by direction of
the Mayor and Recorder!!* Such outrageous
violations of the Constitution need no comment.

You thus see, fellow citizens, how the Slave
power tramples on the *sacredness* of the mail. We
will now show you by figures how and why the
same power has thus far opposed, and successfully
opposed, all reduction of our present enormous
rates of postage.

According to the last report of the Postmaster
General, the excess of revenue over the expenditure
in the Free states is 552,066 dollars ; while the excess of expenditure over the revenue in the Slave
states is 545,262 dollars ; that is, while the Free
states are a GAIN to the department of more than half
a million of dollars, the Slave states are a LOSS to
the department of over half a million of dollars ; in
other words, Northern freemen pay the postage of
Southern slaveholders. Compare our own state,
fellow citizens, with Virginia, and the contrast is
still more striking. In Pennsylvania the excess of
the revenue over the expenditure is 147,409 dollars ; in Virginia the excess of expenditure over the
revenue is 50,777 dollars ; so that our citizens,
besides paying our own postage, pay the postages
of Virginia, and then have enough to make up the
deficiencies of Maryland, South Carolina, and
Mississippi. No wonder the Slave power has
opposed all reduction of rates. The present system
suits them exactly. And what do we get in return

for thus paying their postage? We have told you. We have *our letters opened and our papers burnt.*

3. *Public Lands.*

Whenever there is to be any distribution of money, fellow citizens, the slaveholders always manage to get the "lion's share." This they did in the "Distribution Bill," which was passed in 1841, to distribute the proceeds of the public lands among the several states. They secured their object by having the distribution based upon "federal numbers," that is, according to their representation in Congress, where three-fifths of the slaves are represented, and not according to free population. Supposing the proceeds of the public lands to be three millions of dollars, Pennsylvania, with a free population more than double that of Virginia by 142,349, instead of receiving more than double the amount, will receive 74,521 dollars less ; and with a free population equal to that of Maryland, Virginia and North Carolina, received 94,330 dollars less. Had our Representatives in Congress had any just sense of what is due to the dignity, the honor, and the interests of their own state, they would have withstood, to the very last, a bill so grossly and palpably unjust. And let us tell you, fellow citizens, that you never will have Representatives in Congress of the right character until you make an effort to elect them. To secure the end, you must adopt the means.

4. *Surplus Revenue.*

Of the same character was the Bill passed in 1836, to distribute the surplus revenue in the Treasury of the United States among the several states. The Secretary of the Treasury calculated that there would be twenty-two millions of dollars to be distributed, and that, too, in the words of the Bill, "in proportion to the representation of the states in the Senate and House of Representatives." By this method of distribution the Slave states, with 3,789,674 free inhabitants, received 9,428,580 dollars, while the Free states, with 7,003,239 free inhabitants, received but 12,571,420 dollars. Had our states received in proportion to our number of free inhabitants, instead of twelve millions and a half, we should have received eighteen millions. The state of Virginia received 1,721,090 dollars; Pennsylvania, 2,244,900 dollars; but had the whole amount of surplus revenue been proportioned as it should have been, we should have received 3,125,927 dollars, or nearly one million more. Or, to place the injustice of this measure in a still broader light, a Virginia slaveholder, with an hundred slaves, receives as much as SIXTY-ONE freemen of Pennsylvania. We need make no further comments, fellow citizens, on a Bill so palpably unjust.

5. *Ratio of Representation.*

Immediately after the last Census of the United States had been taken, it became the duty of Con-

gress to fix a new ratio for Representation. The
subject was before the House of Representatives
for a long time, and a variety of numbers were
proposed that should be entitled to one Representative. At last they agreed that there should
be one for every 50,189, which would have given
306 members to the House; and they sent the Bill
to the Senate. That body, however, which, of the
two, has ever been most subservient to the Slave
power, saw that this would not do. They saw
that this Bill would give the Free states a majority
of 68 in the House. They knew, indeed, that
our states must have, in any case, a majority; but
they also knew that they could better manage and
break down a small majority than a large one, and
immediately they set themselves to work to see
how they could weaken us the most. They,
therefore, sent back to the House a Bill, giving
one Representative to every 70,680 of federal
population, and which would *reduce* the House
from its then number, 242 members, to 223; and
give the Free states a majority of 47 instead of 68.
But why that odd number 680 ? We will tell you,
fellow citizens. It deprives the four great states of
the North, namely, Massachusetts, New York,
Pennsylvania, and Ohio of one member each.
Take that number off, and let it be 70,000, and
all the *other* states would have *precisely the same*
number of Representatives. It would injure no
one to take off the 680; but put it on, and it gives

to the great states we have mentioned one Representative less.

And then, too, look at the fractions unrepresented. While all the Slave states have but 140.092, the Free states have 218,678, a difference of 78,586. The fraction of Virginia is 2, that of Pennsylvania is 27,687, besides that she is deprived of one member in the House. And the House, to their shame be it said, concurred in this Bill, so clearly and designedly lessening their influence. Even the correspondent of the "New York Herald" could thus write at the time:—"The Senate Apportionment has robbed the North of at least one quarter of its practical influence in the Union when regarded in its full extent; and the members of the Free states who voted for it have thus yielded and surrendered the rights of their constituents, and violated their trusts."

THE SLAVE POWER THE CHIEF CAUSE OF OUR FINANCIAL EMBARRASSMENTS; OR, IN PLAINER WORDS, OF "HARD TIMES."

1. *By controlling things abroad.*

IF you will take the pains, fellow citizens, to look into our commercial treaties with foreign nations, you will find that the great majority of them are made with reference to the products of Slave labor. All our ambassadors to foreign courts have ever been particularly instructed in this respect. The cry has been continually, *cotton*, COTTON ; *tobacco*, TOBACCO ; *rice*, RICE. For very many years after the formation of our government, wheat and flour, the products of the Free states, constituted the chief articles of our export. We hardly need tell you that these were years of unexampled prosperity to our country. But in later times, and particularly since the signal overthrow of the friends of freedom in the Missouri struggle, down to that ever-to-be-remembered and disgraceful letter of instructions, written by Daniel Webster to Mr. Everett, at London, respecting the slaves shipwrecked in the Creole, the Slave power, by uniting with one or the other of the two great parties of the North, has managed so adroitly, by securing all the important offices of the Government to itself, that the foreign markets for free labor produce have been growing less and less, and those for the products of slave labor have been constantly enlarging. We have seen England, France, Austria, and Russia, one after another, induced, by the incessant persuasions of our General Government, to modify or remove their onerous duties on COTTON and TOBACCO ; while not an effort has been made to induce England to alter her corn-laws ; or to persuade France, or any other European power so to modify their tariffs, as to favor the importation, into those countries, of the wheat, the provisions,* the products of the fisheries, the forests, and the mines, or any of the various manufactures from the Free states of the North or the West.

2. *By controlling things at home.*

Here, fellow citizens, we have to speak of a subject, which we have all, within the last ten years, more or less severely felt—the influence of the Slave power in producing our embarrassments in commerce, in agriculture, and in all the arts and employments of life. Looking always with a most jealous eye upon the prosperity of the North, and knowing that, with the indomitable energies of free labor, it can adapt itself to almost any system, *provided it be permanent*, the object of the Slave power has ever been change, *change*, CHANGE.

Very many years ago foreign commerce found no favor in its eyes, but domestic manufactures were loudly called for. Well, domestic manufactures were established. But scarcely had the North begun to put forth its giant strength in them, when the South felt that its locks must be shorn, and demanded a return to free trade, under the threat of dissolving the Union, unless this demand were complied with. All the changes that have been made in the tariff that have ope-

---

* England has lately made some alteration in her tariff as regards " provisions; " but no thanks to the powers at Washington.

rated unfriendly to Northern interests, (and such changes have taken place every few years,) have been made by the South; and " the great compromiser," Henry Clay, has always managed to "compromise" but one way—*against free*, and FOR SLAVE labor.

But, above all, look at the enormous losses which the North has sustained from its Southern trade. It has found, by its own sad experience, that there is more than one " Grand Gulf" at the South; that the whole South is but ONE GRAND GULF, constantly calling for and swallowing up the free capital of the Free states. This, the failure of the U. S. Bank; this, the losses of thousands of merchants, and manufacturers, and mechanics throughout our Free states, affecting everywhere so injuriously the great farming interests, most conclusively prove.

It is computed that the Slave states owe the Free states, at the lowest estimate, THREE HUNDRED MILLIONS OF DOLLARS; while some have reckoned it as high as FOUR HUNDRED AND FIFTY MILLIONS. In 1837, New York and other cities of the North and East, lost ONE HUNDRED MILLIONS of dollars in Southern debts. In 1838, Maryland, Virginia, and Kentucky lost EIGHTY MILLIONS of dollars, because Mississippi, that "*chivalrous*" state, refused to pay for the slaves she had illegally imported. But this loss fell ultimately on the Free states,

who received in payment for the debts due to
them from the *slave selling* states, paper endorsed
by the banks of the *slave buying* states—the
banks at Mobile, Vicksburg, Grand Gulf, and
New Orleans.

And now, fellow citizens, let us come home to
ourselves. You all remember, too well, the
fall of the United States Bank, and the other
banks in Philadelphia, a few years ago; and how
many banks in the interior, by having more or
less of the stock and other obligations of these
institutions, were materially crippled. And you
remember, too, the utter failure of many of our
best merchants; and the great, though not de-
structive, losses of many more. Why, and whence
all this? We will tell you,—connections with the
Slaveholding states, by speculations in cotton, by
giving long credits to Southern merchants for
goods, and by purchasing the stocks of their banks,
and railroads, and other companies, to enormous
amounts. The United States Bank has now due
to it from the Slave states debts to the amount of
at least TWENTY MILLIONS OF DOLLARS; and the
merchants of Philadelphia, including all who purchased Southern stocks, lost from the year 1834
to 1839, at the lowest estimate, THIRTY MILLIONS
OF DOLLARS, in the Slave states, of which they
will never receive one cent.

Here, then, we have an amount of FIFTY
MILLIONS OF DOLLARS utterly sunk. The dis-

tress which these losses occasioned, you all, fellow citizens, well know; and many, too many, of you most deeply feel. How many a person in the decline of life, who had retired from business, how many an orphan, how many a widow, had their ALL laid up in that *mammoth institution,* in the fullest assurance that it would yield them a sure and regular return while life should last. And at its fall, how much sorrow, how much distress, how much real, bitter, pinching poverty did it bring with it. How many a hearth was made cold and cheerless, how many a mansion made desolate, how many were thrown upon the cold charities of the world. Nor were the losses confined to Philadelphia. By no means. They reached every corner of the State—every log house beyond the mountains. Can FIFTY MILLIONS OF DOLLARS be sunk in a city, the great emporium of trade and commerce—the great receiver and distributor of the products of labor, and the loss not be felt along every road, and highway and canal that leads to it? Can a central, vital function of the body be diseased, and the derangement not be felt throughout every vein and artery of the system? Impossible.

OUR OBJECT.

AND now, fellow citizens, you may ask, what is our object in thus exhibiting to you the alarming influence of the Slave power? Do we wish to excite in your bosoms feelings of hatred against citizens of a common country? Do we wish to array the Free states against the Slave states in hostile strife? NO, fellow citizens, NO, NO. But we wish to show you that, while the Slave states are inferior to us in free population, having not even one half of ours; inferior in morals, being the region of bowie knives and duels, of assassinations and lynch law; inferior in mental attainments, having not one-fourth of the number that can read and write; inferior in intelligence,* having not one-fifth of the number of literary and scientific periodicals; inferior in the products of agriculture and manufactures, of the mines, of the fisheries, and of the forest; inferior, in short, in everything that constitutes the wealth, the honor, the dignity, the stability, the happiness, the true greatness of a nation, it is wrong, it is unjust, it is absurd, that they should have an influence in all the departments of government so entirely dispro-portionate to our own. We would arouse you to your own true interests. We would have you, like men, firmly resolved to maintain your own rights. We would have you say to the South,—

---

* And here, in this connection, we would remark, that if Northern freemen had a proper sense of their own dignity and rights, they would say to every editor of a newspaper or magazine, who cringes to the Slave power, if you choose rather to favor that region so devoid of intelligence, to that region go; and we will support those journals that "know their rights, and knowing dare maintain."

if you choose to hug to your bosom that system
which is continually injuring and impoverishing
you; that system which reduces two millions and
a half of native Americans in your midst to the
most abject condition of ignorance and vice, withholding from them the very key of knowledge;
that system which is at war with every principle
of justice, every feeling of humanity; that system
which makes man the property of man, and per-
petuates that relation from one generation to
another; that system which tramples, continually,
upon a majority of the commandments of the
Decalogue; that system which could not live a
day if it did not give one party supreme control
over the persons, the health, the liberty, the
happiness, the marriage relations, the parental
authority and filial obligations of the other; if
you choose to cling to such a system—cling to it;
but you shall not cross our line; you shall not
bring that foul thing here. We know, and we
here repeat it for the thousandth time, to meet, for
the thousandth time, the calumnies of our enemies,
that while we may present to you every consideration of duty, we have no right, as well as no
power, to alter your State laws. But remember,
that slavery is the mere creature of local or statute
law, and cannot exist out of the region where such
law has force. "It is so *odious*," says Lord
Mansfield, "that nothing can be suffered to support
it but *positive* law."

We would, therefore, say to you again, in the strength of that Constitution under which we live, and which no where countenances slavery, you shall not bring that foul thing here. You shall not force the corrupted, and corrupting blood of that system into every vein and artery of our body politic. You shall not have the controlling power in all the departments of our government at home and abroad. You shall not so negotiate with foreign powers, as to open markets for the products of slave labor alone. You shall not so manage things at home, as every few years to bring bankruptcy upon our country. You shall not, in the apportionment of public moneys, have what you call your "property" represented, and thus get that which, by no right, belongs to you. You shall not have the power to bring your slaves upon our free soil, and take them away at pleasure; nor to reclaim them, when they, panting for liberty, have been able to escape your grasp; for we would have it said of us, as the eloquent Curran said of Britain, the moment the slave touches our soil, " The ground on which he stands is holy, and consecrated to the Genius of UNIVERSAL EMANCIPATION."

Thus, fellow citizens, we come to

THE GREAT OBJECT OF THE LIBERTY PARTY.

IT is, in the words of the Constitution, "TO ESTABLISH JUSTICE ; TO SECURE THE BLESSINGS OF LIBERTY." It is, ABSOLUTE AND UNQUALI-

FIED DIVORCE OF THE GENERAL GOVERNMENT FROM ALL CONNECTION WITH SLAVERY; and we would, therefore, here utter our solemn protest against the nefarious doctrine avowed by HENRY CLAY, in the Senate of the United States, in January, 1839, that " this Government is bound to protect the domestic slave trade." We would say, in the eloquent language of that noble son of freedom, CASSIUS M. CLAY, of Kentucky, " Let the whole North in a mass, in conjunction with the patriotic of the South, withdraw the moral sanction and legal power of the Union from the sustainment of slavery." We would employ every CONSTITUTIONAL means to eradicate it from our entire country, because it would be for the highest welfare of our entire country. We would have liberty established in the District, and in all the Territories. We would put a stop to the internal slave trade, pronounced, even by Thomas Jefferson Randolph, of Virginia, to be " worse and more odious than the foreign slave trade itself." We would, in the words of the Constitution, have " the citizens of each state have all the privileges and immunities of citizens in the several states;" and not, for the color of their skin, be subjected to every indignity, and abuse, and wrong, and even imprisonment.*

---

* Read the memorial of citizens of Boston to the House of Representatives, on the imprisonment of free citizens of Massachusetts by the authorities of Savannah, Charleston, and New Orleans.

We would have equal taxation. We would have the seas free. We would have a free and secure post office. We would have liberty of speech and of the press, which the Constitution guarantees to us. We would have our members in Congress utter their thoughts freely, without threats from the pistol or the bowie knife. We would have the right of petition most sacredly regarded. We would secure to every man what the Constitution secures, " the right of trial by jury." We would do what we can for the encouragement and improvement of the colored race, and restore to them that inestimable right of which they have been so meanly, as well as unjustly, deprived—the RIGHT OF SUFFRAGE. We would look to the best interests of the country, and the *whole* country, and not legislate for the good of an Oligarchy, the most arrogant that ever lorded it over an insulted people.*
We would have our commercial treaties with foreign nations regard the interests of the Free states. We would provide safe, adequate, and permanent markets for the produce of free labor. And, when reproached with slavery, we would be able to say to the world, with an open front and a clear conscience, our General Government has nothing

---

* The slaveholders, at most, do not number over 250,000 ; not so many as there are inhabitants in the city and districts of Philadelphia. How humiliating that such a set of men should govern such a country.

to do with it, either to promote, to sustain, to defend, to sanction, or to approve.

Thus, fellow citizens, you see our objects. You may now ask, by what means we hope to attain them. We answer, by

POLITICAL ACTION.

What is political action? It is, *acting in a manner appropriate to those objects which we wish to secure through the agency of the different departments of Government.* He, for instance, who desires Congress to charter a national bank, or to pass a highly restrictive tariff, will do what he can to send to Congress such men as are known to be favorable to those objects. So he who is interested for the freedom of millions of the human race; who desires that our general government may be entirely divorced from all connection with slavery; who wishes to see our country governed by "just men," will, if consistent, adopt measures appropriate to secure such ends. What are those measures? There is but one answer. The only way in which he can act *constitutionally,* is to go to the ballot-box, and there, silently and unostentatiously, deposit a vote for such men as will do what they can to carry out those principles which he has so much at heart. This is POLITICAL ACTION, or action in political affairs; and is as pure, in itself, as action in domestic, or mercantile, or ecclesiastical affairs. We grant that not the

D

purest associations have been connected with the phrase, because good men have too often stood aloof from political action, and have left the great affairs of government to be managed by not the most worthy ;—by those who make politics a sort of trade.

But we now, fellow citizens, propose to you a sort of political action in which you may most ardently engage without being soiled. It is the same political action which was enjoined more than three thousand years ago. " Moreover thou shalt provide out of all the people able men, such as fear God, men of truth, hating covetousness, and place such men over them to be rulers."* This, fellow citizens, we have done, and this we ever intend to do; and in this action we now invite your aid.

In saying this, we do not intend to underrate moral suasion. Far, very far, from it. None can value it more highly. We are always using it, and we hope ever to use it till slavery is overthrown. Moral power is, indeed, *the* great power. But as in most other cases, so here, this power must have a lever which it can grasp and wield, in order to be effectual. That lever is POLITICAL ACTION. Why? Plainly, because Slavery is the creature of " political action," and how else than by " political action" can it be abolished? The laws that sustain slavery are not the laws of God, but in total

---

* Exodus xviii. 21.

violation of His laws. Neither did they make themselves; and they cannot annul themselves. They were made by men, and by men only can they be repealed. But they were made by selfish, unjust men; by men regardless of the rights of their fellow-men. They must therefore be repealed by men of a character totally different: by men who regard justice and equal rights: by men who have no sympathy with the proud oppressor: by men who will dare to do right; who will meet any obloquy, and face any danger in the course where duty leads. And how are such men to be placed in office? We answer, of course, BY VOTES, fellow citizens. There is no other constitutional way. The case is as clear as any axiom in mathematics.

We ask, then, how can any good man—any true friend of his country's best interests—any lover of justice and humanity—for a moment doubt what his duty herein is? Will he withdraw from all action in the questions of the deepest public interest, and leave everything to be managed by those who make politics a trade? And if he makes no effort, in the way the Constitution provides, to remedy great evils, with what face, we ask, can he complain of the continuance of those evils? But you may ask why we adopt a

SEPARATE ORGANIZATION.

WE answer, because we believe this to be the

only effectual mode to accomplish our object.   For years and years we tried both the two great political parties; but all in vain.   Henry Clay himself said in the U. S. Senate, "It is not true, and I REJOICE that it is not true, that *either* of the two great parties in this country has any *design or aim at abolition*.   I should *deeply lament* if it were true."   Of the great number of candidates, therefore, whom we would question as to their views in relation to our great objects, some would not answer at all; some would answer in a manner insulting to our feelings ; and some would answer, like the oracle at Delphi, as profound as unmeaning. A very few would answer favorably to secure our votes, and then, after they were elected by our votes, would turn around and laugh at our credulity.   A sense of what is due to ourselves and to the best good of our country, has compelled us, therefore, to the course we have taken.

At the approaching election, fellow citizens, you will have before you the candidates of three parties, from which you are to choose.   The candidate of the Whig party for the Presidency is

HENRY CLAY.

IT is painful to us, fellow citizens, at any time, to speak against the character of any one.   But in a case like this, when most unworthy candidates are presented for your suffrage by two of the parties, feeling must yield to duty, and we must tell you *why* they are unworthy of your confidence.

There are some features of the moral character of HENRY CLAY which we have not the least desire to discuss. From the time that he first entered upon public life at Washington, until within a very few years, unless common fame has done him the grossest injustice, his moral character could not but meet the reprobation of every good man. Had he given any evidence of sincere repentance, we would be the last even to allude to these things. That he is utterly unworthy of the suffrages of the friends of liberty, however, we need hardly tell you. That a man who will say in a speech before the Colonization Society, that he is utterly opposed to all emancipation of the slaves, either "immediate or gradual, without their removal;" that a man who exerted all his influence for the admission of Missouri into the Union, as a slave state;* that a man who declared in the Senate of the United States, February 9, 1839, that " that is property which the law declares to be property "—" that two hun-

---

* As if the deed itself was not bad enough, he must add to its wickedness, the wickedness of violating the Fourth Commandment. " It was in this very Chamber, Senator Holmes, of Maine, presiding in a committee of the Senate, and I in a committee of twenty-four of the House of Representatives, ON A SABBATH DAY, that the terms were adjusted by which the Missouri compromise was effected." *Speech, Feb.* 23, 1835. In his recent Southern tour, he has been guilty of the same sin to a most shameless extent.

dred years of legislation have SANCTIFIED negro slaves AS PROPERTY;" who, in the same speech, pronounced the opinion of Madison, that "man cannot hold property in man," to be a " visionary dogma;" and who had the awful blasphemy to compare men, held as slaves, with other " LIVE STOCK;" that such a man has no claims to a free-man's vote we need, certainly, take no pains to prove.

But that which should render HENRY CLAY still more odious, if possible, in the eyes of every good man, is the fact that HE IS THE GREAT DUELLIST OF THE LAND. The first affair of murder in which he was engaged was with Colonel Daviess, of Kentucky, in 1805. A chal-lenge was given and accepted, and both parties were proceeding to the work of death, when the seconds brought about a reconciliation. His mur-derous intention, however, remained. The second duel was with Humphrey Marshall, also of Ken-tucky, in 1808. They exchanged shots three times, and both parties were slightly wounded, when they declared themselves " satisfied." The third duel was with John Randolph, then Senator from Virginia, when Mr. Clay was Secretary of State under John Quincy Adams. At the second shot Mr. Clay's ball passed through Mr. Ran-dolph's dress, when both parties declared a cessa-tion of hostilities. In these instances, indeed, he did not kill his antagonists; not, however, from

want of intention, but from want of skill. But the
fourth affair of murder, in which Mr. Clay has
been engaged, is that which ought to stamp his
name with lasting infamy; for it was he that
penned the challenge, and arranged the terms of
that fatal duel which, in February, 1838, sent
Jonathan Cilley, a member of Congress from the
State of Maine, to his grave. Mr. Wise, in his
place in Congress, declared, that Henry Clay
" governed all the preliminaries" of that murderous
affray; that he (Mr. Wise) " protested against the
language of the challenge, which closed the door to
an adjustment of the difficulty, but *was over-ruled
by Mr. Clay;*" and that, " had the principals and
the two seconds been free to act in this matter, not
a shot would have been fired."* His hands, therefore, are stained with the blood of the murdered
Cilley, and all the waters of the ocean cannot wash
it out. Lastly, as late as 1841, he showed as much
eagerness for murder as ever; for when, after that
bitter war of words between himself and Mr. King,
of Alabama, in the U. S. Senate, Mr. Clay pro-
nouncing what Mr. King had said to be " unjust,
false, and cowardly," intending thereby to provoke
a challenge, that he might have the choice of
weapons, Dr. Linn, of Missouri, handed a note to
Mr. Clay, the latter said, before opening it, in tones

---

* See Globe and National Intelligencer of January 29,
1842, and Pennsylvanian of January 31, 1842.

of most embittered rage, "a challenge, I suppose; I ACCEPT IT;" thus showing that age had not cooled his ardor for the work of death.

Thus, fellow citizens, you have before you the candidate of the Whig party for the Presidency. The law of Pennsylvania, passed March 31, 1806, reads thus: " Any person fighting a duel, challenging, or accepting a challenge, shall pay the sum of 500 dollars, and suffer one year's imprisonment at hard labor, in the same manner as convicted felons are now punished." You therefore see, that, had Henry Clay been tried by our laws, he would, at three several times, have been sent to our Penitentiary.

We now ask you to listen to the warnings of some of the wisest and best men in our land. Says the distinguished Dr. Beecher, in a sermon delivered about two years after Hamilton was murdered by Aaron Burr,—

" The inconsistency of VOTING for a duellist is glaring. To profess attachment for liberty, and VOTE for a man whose principles and practice are alike hostile to liberty, is a farce too ridiculous to be acted by freemen.

" In our prayers we request that God would bestow upon us good rulers ; ' just men, walking in the fear of God.' But by voting for the duellist we demonstrate the insincerity of such prayers.

" But you may say, if I do not vote for the man on my side, will not this be helping his antagonist, and will not this be as bad as if I voted directly ? No . . It is certainly a different thing whether a vile man comes into power BY your agency, or IN SPITE of it. But suppose the duellist in all respects, excepting this crime, is a better man than his opponent; of two evils may we not choose the least? Yes, of two natural evils you may; if you must lose a finger or an arm, cut off the finger; but of two sinful things you may choose neither, and therefore you may not vote for one bad man, a MUR-DERER, to keep out another bad man. It is 'to do evil that good may come,' and of all who do this, the Apostle declares 'their damnation is just.'

"And now let me ask you, in conclusion, will you any longer, either deliberately or thoughtlessly, VOTE for these guilty men? Will you renounce allegiance to your Maker, and cast the Bible behind your back? Will you confide in men void of the fear of God, and destitute of moral principle? Will you intrust LIFE to MURDERERS and LIBERTY to DESPOTS? Will you *bestow your suffrage,* when you know that, by withholding it, you may arrest this deadly evil—when the remedy is so easy, so entirely in your power; and when God, if you do not punish these guilty men, will most inevitably punish you?"

Says Dr. Sprague, of Albany, in a sermon preached after Cilley was murdered by Graves,—

"Let every citizen, when he goes to the BALLOT-BOX, inquire whether it will be safe to put his dearest interests into the keeping of a MURDERER; and let him resolve, as he would keep a conscience void of offence, that no man who GIVES or ACCEPTS a challenge, shall EVER have his vote."

With reference to the assertion often made, that "we must choose the least of two evils," Dr. Bushnell, of Hartford, thus most solemnly exclaims:—

"Merciful God! has it come to this, that in choosing rulers, we are simply to choose whether the nation shall be governed by seven devils or ten? Is this the alternative offered to our consciences and our liberties? There never was a maxim more corrupt, more totally bereft of principle, than this—that between bad men, you are to choose the least wicked of the two."

What now, fellow citizens, shall be thought of those who, within a few weeks, have been running, in thousands, to hear the harangues of GRAVES the MURDERER, and who would elevate to the Presidency THE GREAT DUELLIST OF THE LAND?

The candidate of the Democratic party is

JAMES K. POLK.

In the first edition of this Address, fellow-citizens, you will remember that the name of Martin Van Buren was inserted in this place. He was evidently the decided favorite of the great majority of his party at the North; and no one doubted that he would receive the nomination of the Convention which was to assemble at Baltimore. Well, the Convention met. The Slave power insisted that two-thirds of the votes should be necessary to constitute a choice; northern DEMOCRATS yielded, as usual, to their masters; when lo! Mr. Van Buren, who at first had 146 out of 266 votes, is finally rejected, and James K. Polk, of Tennessee, receives the vote of the Convention.

But what had Mr. Van Buren done to displease the slaveholders? We will tell you: He had written a letter—the most creditable document he ever wrote—against the immediate annexation of Texas; that scheme of the Slave power to extend its nefarious "institution." He, therefore, received but TWELVE votes from the Slave states, and a slaveholder is brought forward, who is an earnest advocate of Texas annexation, with all its attendant wickedness and consequent calamities; and who has distinguished himself in nothing but in the tyranny with which he exercised his authority for four years, while Speaker of the House, in enforcing the " gag rule," to an extent that not even its notorious author had ever contemplated.

And now we would ask, with all earnestness, how much longer, Citizens of the Free states, are ye to remain in vassalage to the slaveholding demagogues of the South? How much longer will you do the bidding of that mere handful of men, who, with the words of DEMOCRACY on their lips, are not only themselves trampling upon the dearest rights of two and a half millions of people in their own region, but have left no arts untried to make you their " allies" in support of their wicked system? Democrats of the North! ye who possess some self-respect, how much longer will you submit to these things? Answer at the ballot-box; and let the insolent " overseers" know, in a language which they will understand, that they may rule *slaves*, but shall not rule FREEMEN.

We now present to you our own candidate,

JAMES GILLESPIE BIRNEY,

Of Michigan, and invite your strictest scrutiny into his character, and his qualifications for the high office for which we have nominated him. Born in Kentucky, in 1792, a graduate of Princeton College, in 1810, and a Student of Law, at Philadelphia, he began the practice of his profession at Danville, his native place, and subsequently pursued it at Huntsville, Alabama. We have no space to go into the particulars of his life. His early attention to the subject of Slavery; his acceptance of the agency of the American Colonization Society, for the Southern states, as a means by which he thought he might do good to the slave; his subsequent convictions of the utter inadequacy of that bubble scheme to effect the alleged object; his long and most able letter of resignation as Agent, and as Vice-President of the Society, in which he makes the just remark, " we are *living down* the foundation principles of our happy institutions;" his noble act of giving freedom to all his own slaves; his efforts, against abuse and obloquy and threats of personal violence, to establish a free press in Cincinnati; the great ability he displayed in conducting that press; his speeches and essays and constitutional arguments on the subject of slavery, all these incidents of his life, and many more as creditable that might be named, give abundant evidence of his ample qualifications for the highest office in our government. But his talents and attainments, however great, would be nothing in our estimation, if they were not accompanied by something higher, purer, nobler. It is his stern integrity of character ; it is his high moral courage, it is his devoted and consistent piety, that make JAMES GILLESPIE BIRNEY eminently deserving the vote of every good man.

Our candidate for the Vice-Presidency, THOMAS MORRIS, of Ohio, is one also in every way worthy of your confidence. While to his moral character no exceptions can be taken, in his public career he has shown himself to be a *true* Democrat by his regard for the rights of *the people* and the *whole people.* After that notorious anti-abolition speech of Henry Clay, to which we have before referred, Thomas Morris, of Ohio, belonging to the so-called Democratic party, presented a preamble and a series of resolutions to the Senate, drawn up with great ability, to meet the sophistry and the declamation of the Kentucky senator. He knew that to act thus would be to lose his position with his own party ; but he took the course which duty, not self-interest, pointed out, and at the next election he was left at home to enjoy the richer rewards of an approving conscience ; for

> " More true joy Marcellus exiled feels,
>   Than Cæsar with a Senate at his heels."

Our candidate for Governor is

DR. FRANCIS JULIUS LEMOYNE,

Of Washington county. Of him we need say but little, as he is well known throughout the State, as much for his pure and elevated character, as for his distinguished intellectual abilities. Of strict integrity himself, he would leave no honest efforts untried that our State should have, at home and abroad, the same character for integrity, *by the just payment of all our debts.* True, he has fought no battles, but those of moral principle in the cause of human rights. But the time has nearly gone by, we trust, when the fact of a man's having been engaged in one or more wars, shall be thought to make him any better qualified for filling the chair of State.

Such, fellow citizens, are the candidates which we present to you. Into their characters, and into the characters of all whom the Liberty Party, now or hereafter, may nominate for office, we invite your strictest scrutiny. If they be not found such as must meet the approbation of every good man who desires to see the highest offices in our country filled by "just men, ruling in the fear of God;" men who will be a "terror to evil doers, and a praise to them that do well;" do not give them your suffrage. But if they be, come and help us to put them in. As to the probabilities of our success, we have everything to encourage us, not only in the JUSTICE, but also in the

PROGRESS OF OUR CAUSE.

THE scenes of mob violence that occurred in the city of Boston, in 1835, when those who spoke

publicly against slavery were threatened with
every indignity, are well known. Now the Liberty
Party hold their meetings in " old Faneuil Hall,"
the " cradle of Liberty," and that immense room
is crowded with eager listeners. A daily Liberty
paper, also, conducted with signal talent, is published in that city; while the vote of Massachusetts, from a few hundred in 1841, has reached
to nearly 9000 in 1843. In 1836, a mob at
Cincinnati tore down the press, and hunted for
the life of *our candidate for the Presidency*, and
assailed with personal violence others well known
as friends of the cause. Now there is published in
that city, also, a daily paper, which, with consum-
mate ability, advocates our principles. In 1837,
resolutions from the state of Massachusetts, on the
subject of slavery, were thrown by Congress, with
contempt, upon the table; now, resolutions from
the same state are referred to a large committee,
of which the great champion of the right of
petition is chairman. The majority in Congress
against receiving all petitions on the subject of
slavery, at first very large, has been growing less
and less every year; until, at last, the " gag rule,"
as it is called, was lately carried but by barely one
vote. In 1837, Dr. Crandall, of New York, was
thrown into prison, in the District of Columbia,
for having anti-slavery pamphlets in his trunk.
Now, a voice breaks forth from the dark walls of
a prison in that very spot; the sound penetrates

the doors of the Capitol; and the petition to
Congress, from a colored man, to interpose in his
behalf, is referred, by a large majority, to the Committee on the Judiciary. In 1840, the first year
of the organization of the Liberty Party, our vote
for President was hardly 7000 in all the states;
while the last year, even for state officers, it
amounted to upwards of 60,000 : thus more than
doubling itself every successive year. The returns
that have been received of a few elections this
Spring show a still greater increase. New Hampshire, which last Fall gave only 3594 votes, has
this Spring given about 6000. It requires but
little arithmetic to see how soon, at this rate, our
cause will be triumphant. Every day we are receiving, in all the Free states, large accessions to
our numbers, of true and honest hearts ; while we
hear from the Slave states themselves, voices all
around, to encourage us in our labors. In Delaware
many of its best citizens are interested in the cause,
and lately held a conference to adopt measures for
the abolition of slavery in that state. In Maryland
the infamous slaveholders' convention was an eminent instance how " God makes the wrath of man
to praise him," as it doubtless advanced the cause
of human freedom in that state very many years ;
for an able weekly paper is now published in Baltimore that takes strong anti-slavery ground. In
Virginia we receive the most cheering intelligence,
that, in a number of counties, systematic efforts are

making to circulate anti-slavery publications, and to spread anti-slavery principles. In Tennessee a regular anti-slavery society has been established. In Kentucky one gentleman writes us, "The Liberty Party is destined to be the most powerful auxiliary in the hands of Providence for the overthrow of American slavery;" while that noble champion of human rights, Cassius M. Clay, by his letters and speeches, and unceasing personal efforts, is gaining for himself a name that will grow brighter and brighter as time rolls on.

Thus far at home. But if we look abroad, we find quite as much to gladden our hearts. The happy workings of emancipation in the British West Indies have exceeded the most sanguine expectations of its warmest friends. The order and industry that there universally prevail—the wonderful improvement in morals, in education, and in everything indicative of a nation's prosperity, are all clear manifestations of the blessing of God that attends an effort of justice and philanthropy. The Emperor of Russia has already done much, and means to do still more, for ameliorating the condition of his serfs. France and Holland will, doubtless, soon take the same steps with their colonial possessions that Great Britain has with hers. The Bey of Tunis, even, has abolished the internal slave trade throughout his dominions, and has himself set to his people the noble example of giving liberty to all his own slaves, and of requiring

E

all the officers of his court to do likewise; while Mexico and the Republics of South America are determined that their practice shall be consistent with their avowed principles of liberty. Our country, as you thus see, fellow citizens, must therefore move soon in the great work, or we shall be left alone in our disgrace, with no one to sympathize with us, no one to countenance us in our course—a course as inconsistent with our professions, as it is disgraceful, and odious, and wicked in itself.

Come, then, men of Pennsylvania, citizens of the same state as Franklin, and Rush, and Wilson, and the Morrises, who thought as we think, and who, were they now living, would doubtless act as we are now acting,—come and join us in this good work. Join us, to use such moral means as to correct public sentiment throughout the region where slavery exists, and to impress upon the people of the Free states a manly sense of their own rights. Join us, to place "just men" in all our public offices; men whose example a whole people may safely imitate. Join us, to free our General Government from the ignominious reproach of slavery; to restore to our country those principles which our fathers so laboured to establish; and to hand these principles down afresh to successive generations. It is the cause of truth, of humanity, and of God, to which we invite your aid. It is a cause of which you never need be ashamed. Living, you may be thankful, and dying, you may be thankful, for having labored in it. We have, as co-laborers with us, the noblest allies that man can wish. Within, we have the deepest convictions of conscience; the clearest deductions of reason; and, all over the world, wherever man is found, the first, the most ardent longings of the human soul. Without, we have the happiness of nearly three millions of the human race; the honor, as well as the best interests of our whole country; and the universal consent of all good men, whose moral vision is not obscured by the mists of a low, misguided selfishness: while we seem to hear, as it were, the voices of the great and the good, the patriot and the philanthropist, of a past generation, calling to us, and cheering us on. But, above all these, and beyond all these, we have with us the highest attributes of God, JUSTICE and MERCY. With such allies, and in such a cause, who can doubt on which side the victory will ultimately rest.

May He who guides the destinies of nations, and without whose aid "they labor in vain that build," so incline your hearts to exert your whole influence to place in all our public offices just and good men, that our country may be preserved, her best interests advanced, and her institutions, free in reality as in name, handed down to the latest posterity.

Signed on behalf of the Eastern State Committee, and by their direction,

CHARLES DEXTER CLEVELAND,

Chairman.

Approved by the Western State Committee,

RUSSELL ERRETT, Chairman.

CINCINNATI ADDRESS.

PREFATORY REMARKS.

S soon as the following Address appeared, I was struck, as indeed all who read it were, with its great eloquence and power; but I felt that its influence would be, comparatively, very much limited in consequence both of the form and of the mediums in which it appeared,—in solid columns, and in two or three anti-slavery papers of but small circulation. I, therefore, wrote to the author, asking of him the permission to divide it into appropriate headings, to add statistical notes corroborative of its general statements, and to have it stereotyped in a pamphlet form. In reply, he gave me full liberty to do with it whatever I thought would be best for the great cause we both had so much at heart. Accordingly, after making such sub-divisions as I thought appropriate, and adding such statistical notes as I thought would fully confirm the assertions of the Address as to the alarming encroachments, as well as the baleful influence of the Slave power, I was enabled, by the generous contributions of a few friends, to have it stereotyped, and to print twenty thousand copies. These were soon disposed of; and so many were subsequently ordered from different parts of the country, that not less than ONE HUNDRED THOUSAND in all were printed and distributed ; it being pronounced by many as "decidedly the most efficient campaign document the Liberty Party could use."

Since that time the author has, as is well known, risen to high political and judicial distinction. But nothing that he has done or written in these positions will place him any higher in the estimation of posterity than this noble Address, *when the time and circumstances in which it was written are considered.* Had he then gone with the so-called "Democratic" party, he might soon have filled almost any office of trust or honor he might desire. But he chose to come out from it and to be separate, preferring truth and righteousness with private life, rather than any public elevation based on falsehood and wrong. The result has been, that at this present time he has awarded to him, by the very best people in every part of our land, a confidence in his wisdom, ability, and integrity of character exceeded by that in no other public man now living.

C. D. C.

THE ADDRESS OF THE SOUTHERN AND WESTERN LIBERTY CONVENTION.

NOTE.

I WOULD not, of course, thus republish this Address of my early college friend without his approbation. Accordingly, in the latter part of 1865 I wrote to him on the subject. He replied, with characteristic kindness, in favor of my design, saying, in substance, that he would like to see the two Addresses bound together in print as their authors were in friendship. Pressing literary avocations, however, and health not the most robust, prevented me from giving my attention to the matter at that time. But having come abroad for my health in June, 1866, and having now, in the Spring of 1867, a little leisure in this great metropolis, I have thought it a very favorable opportunity for completing the work so long contemplated.

C. D. C.

LONDON, May, 1867.

THE ADDRESS OF THE
SOUTHERN AND WESTERN LIBERTY CONVENTION,

HELD AT CINCINNATI, JUNE 11 AND 12, 1845,[*]

TO THE PEOPLE OF THE UNITED STATES.

WITH NOTES BY A CITIZEN OF
PENNSYLVANIA.

HAVING assembled in Convention as friends of Constitutional Liberty, who believe the practice of slaveholding to be inconsistent with the fundamental principles of Republicanism, of Religion, and of Humanity, we think it our duty to declare frankly to you, our fellow citizens, the views which we hold, the principles by which we are governed, and the objects which we desire, by your co-operation, to accomplish. We ask and expect from you a candid and respectful hearing. We are not a band of fanatics, as some foolishly imagine, and others slanderously assert, bent on the overthrow of all Govern-

---

[*] See note 1 in Appendix.

ment and all Religion. We are citizens of the United States, having our homes in the West and the Southwest, some in the Slave states, and some in the Free, bound to our country by the most endearing ties and the most solemn obligations, filled with the most ardent desires for her prosperity and glory, and resolved, so far as in us lies, to carry forward and perfect the great work of individual, social, and civil elevation which our fathers nobly began.

THE REVOLUTION.

THE American Revolution was not a mere political accident. It was an inevitable result of a long train of causes, all conspiring to make men impatient of oppression. It was a necessary battle in the progress of the great conflict between Despotism and Freedom, between the Aristocratic and the Democratic principle.

Our fathers so regarded it. They claimed for themselves no new or peculiar rights : they only demanded security in the enjoyment of those rights to which, as descendants of Englishmen, they were entitled under the Great Charter : to which, as men, they were entitled under the grant of the Creator. They asserted the equal right of all men to the immunities which they claimed for themselves. It was impossible that they should not see and feel the gross inconsistency of the practice of slaveholding with their avowed political faith. The writings of the Revolutionary period afford the amplest evidence

that they did perceive and feel it. But slavery was
already in the country, interwoven with domestic
habits, pecuniary interests, and legal rights. It ex-
isted under the sanction of the laws of the several
colonies beyond the reach of the direct legislation
of Congress. The consequences of an immediate
affranchisement of the enslaved were, also, generally
dreaded. Our fathers, therefore, confined themselves to general declarations of the great doctrine
of equal rights, which lies at the basis of all just
government; and without directly interfering with
the legislation of any particular member of the con-
federacy, endeavoured to establish the national Government and Policy upon such principles as would
bring about, at length, the desired result of Universal Freedom.

We solicit your particular attention, fellow citizens, to this statement. It has been the practice of
many to represent the American government as the
patron and guardian of slavery. Some have even
dared to say that it was the purpose of the foun-
ders of the government that it should fulfil this
office. We join issue with all such persons. We
denounce all such representations as libels upon
the great men who won and bequeathed to us the
precious heritage of Free Institutions. We insist
that from the assembling of the First Congress in
1774, until its final organization under the existing
constitution in 1789, the American Government
was anti-slavery in its character and policy.

The importance of this position, and the probability that this address will be read by some who have not examined it, justify the appropriation of some space to the proof of it.

FIRST CONGRESS.

WE therefore invite your attention to a memorable act of the First Congress, which assembled in 1774. The Non-Importation, Non-Consumption, and Non-Exportation Agreement of that illustrious body, signed in their individual and representative capacities, by the delegates of all the represented colonies, and promulgated to the world as the solemn act of United America, contained this remarkable clause :—" We will neither import nor purchase any slave imported after the first day of December next : after which time we will wholly discontinue the slave trade, and neither be concerned in it ourselves, nor will we hire our vessels or sell our commodities or manufactures to those who may be concerned in it." The entire agreement of which this clause was part was not, indeed, intended to be of perpetual obligation : yet the singularly emphatic phraseology of this part of it manifests clearly enough the understanding of the delegates as to the obligation they assumed for themselves and for the country. It was, in fact, a deliberate national vow and covenant against all traffic in human beings, and was so understood by the people at large. Virginia proceeded, soon after, to abolish the slave trade by a solemn act of legislation, and her example was followed by all or nearly all the States.

DECLARATION OF INDEPENDENCE.

Two years afterwards, the Declaration of Independence was promulgated to the world. In a single sentence of this great Act, our fathers imbodied the fundamental principles on which they proposed to establish the free government of the United States. " We hold these truths to be self-evident; that all men are created equal; that they are endowed by their Creator with certain inalienable rights; that among these are life, liberty, and the pursuit of happiness." In these words, for the first time in the history of the world, was the doctrine of the inalienable RIGHT of every man to life, liberty, and the pursuit of happiness, solemnly proclaimed AS THE BASIS OF A NATIONAL POLITICAL FAITH. This declaration pledged its authors, and the nation which made it its own, by adoption, to eternal hostility to every form of despotism and oppression. With this declaration inscribed upon their banners, they went into the war of the Revolution, invoking the attestation of the " Supreme Judge of the world" to the rectitude of their purposes.

After a protracted and dubious struggle, the independence of the American Republic was at length achieved, and the attention of Congress was turned to the establishment and extension of free institutions. Beyond the Alleghany Mountains, then the western limit of civilization, stretched a vast territory, untrodden except by the savage, but destined, in the hope and faith of the patriots of the Revolution, to be the seat of mighty states. To this territory, during the war just terminated, various States had set up conflicting claims : while the Congress had urged upon all, the cession of their several pretensions for the common good. The recommendations of Congress prevailed. Among the States which signalized their patriotism by the cession of claims to Western Territory, Virginia was pre-eminently distinguished, both by the magnitude of her grant and the spirit in which it was made. The claim of Virginia comprehended almost all that is now Ohio, Indiana, and Illinois. She yielded it all, almost with no other condition than that the territory should be disposed of for the common benefit, and finally erected into Republican States. The absence of all stipulations in behalf of slavery in these cessions, and especially in that of Virginia, furnishes strong evidence of the prevalence of anti-slavery sentiment at that day. But the action of Congress, in relation to the territory thus acquired, supplies decisive proof.

ORDINANCE OF 1787.

It was in 1787 that Congress promulgated the celebrated Ordinance for the Government of the Territory north-west of the river Ohio. In this ordinance, for the purpose of " extending the fun-

damental principles of civil and religious liberty;
* * to fix and establish those principles as the basis
of all laws, constitutions, and governments, which
for ever thereafter should be formed in said territory," Congress established " certain articles of
compact between the original States and the people
and States in the territory to remain for ever
unalterable, unless by common consent." One of
these articles of compact declared that there should
be " neither slavery nor involuntary servitude in
the territory, otherwise than in the punishment of
crimes;" providing, however, that the right of
retaking fugitives from service should be preserved
to the citizens of the original States. This ordinance was adopted by the unanimous vote of all
the States, there being but a single individual negative, which was given by a member from New
York. Upon the question of excluding slavery,
we may fairly assume that there was entire unanimity.

It seems to us impossible to conceive of a more
significant indication of National Policy. The
Congress was about to fix for ever the relation of
five future States to the question of slavery.
Under the influence of the liberal opinions of 1776,
Massachusetts, New Hampshire, Connecticut,
Rhode Island, Vermont and Pennsylvania, had
already abolished or had taken measures for abo-
lishing slavery within their limits. It was expected
that other Atlantic States would follow their

F

example. The creation of five non-slaveholding
States in the West would evidently secure a permanent majority on the side of Freedom against
Slavery. There was, at that time, no other national
territory out of which slaveholding States could be
carved: nor was there any thought of acquiring
territory with such an object. And yet the votes of
Delaware, Maryland, Virginia, North Carolina,
South Carolina and Georgia were given, and
unanimously given, for the positive exclusion of
slavery from all the vast region now possessed by
Ohio, Indiana, Illinois, Michigan and Wisconsin,
and for the virtual restriction of the right of
reclaiming fugitive servants to cases of escape from
the original States. There was very little compromise here. There was clear, unqualified, decisive
action in the fulfilment and in renewal of the solemn
pledge given in 1774, reiterated in 1776, and in
pursuance of the settled national policy of restricting slavery to the original States, and of excluding
it from all national territory and from all new
States.

It is to be borne in mind that neither in this
ordinance, nor in the national acts which preceded
it, did the Congress undertake to legislate upon the
actual personal relations of the inhabitants of the
original States. They sought to impress upon the
national character and the national policy the stamp
of Liberty ; but they did not, so far as we can see,
attempt to interfere with the internal arrangements

of any State, however inconsistent those arrangements might be with that character and policy. They expected, however, and they had reason to expect, that slavery would be excluded from all places of national jurisdiction, and that whatever in the arrangements of particular States savoured of despotism and oppression, and especially that the system of slavery, which concentrates in itself the whole essence and all the attributes of despotism and oppression, would give way before the steady action of the national faith and the national policy.

Such was the state of opinion when the Convention for framing the Constitution of the United States assembled. The ordinance of 1787, which was the most significant and decisive expression of this opinion, was promulgated while the Constitution-Convention was in session. The Constitution, therefore, is to be examined with reference to the public acts which preceded it, and the prevalent popular sentiment.

THE CONSTITUTION.

And the first thing which arrests the attention of the inquirer is the remarkable preamble which is prefixed to the operative clauses of the instrument, in which the objects to be attained by it are particularly enumerated.—These are, " to form a more perfect union, establish justice, ensure domestic tranquillity, provide for the common defence, promote the general welfare, and secure the blessings of liberty." It would be singular, indeed, if a constitution adopted for such objects, and under such circumstances, should be found to contain guaranties of slavery. We should expect, on the contrary, that, although the national government created by it, might not be directly authorized to act upon the slavery already existing in the States, all power to create or continue the system by national sanction would be carefully withheld, and some safeguards would be provided against its further extension. And such, in our judgment, was the true effect of the Constitution. We are not prepared to deny, on the one hand, that several clauses of the instrument were intended to refer to slaves ; nor to admit, on the other, all the consequences which the friends of slavery would deduce from these clauses. We abstain from these questions. It is enough for our purpose, that it seems clear that neither the framers of the Constitution, nor the people who adopted it, intended to violate the pledges given in the Covenant of 1774, in the Declaration of 1776, in the Ordinance of 1787; that they did not purpose to confer on Congress or the General Government any power to establish, or continue, or sanction slavery anywhere; that, if they did not intend to authorize direct national legislation for the removal of the slavery existing in particular States under their local laws, they did intend to keep the action of the national government free from all connection with the system ; to discountenance and discourage it in the States ; and to favour the abolition of it by State authority—a result, then, generally expected ; and, finally, to provide against its further extension by confining the power to acquire new territory, and admit new States to the General Government, the line of whose policy was clearly marked out by the ordinance and preceding public acts.

We cannot think that any unprejudiced student of the Constitution, examining it in the light of precedent action, and contemporary opinion, can arrive at any other conclusion than this. No amendment of the Constitution would be needed to adapt it to the new condition of things, were every State in the Union to abolish slavery forthwith. There is not a line of the instrument which refers to slavery as a national institution, to be upheld by national law. On the contrary, every clause which ever has been or can be construed as referring to slavery, treats it as the creature of State law, and dependent wholly upon State law for its existence and continuance. So careful were the framers of the Constitution to negative all implied sanction of slaveholding, that not only were the terms " slave," " slavery," and " slaveholding" excluded, but even the word " servitude," which was at first inserted to express the condition, under the local law, of the persons who were to be delivered up, should they escape from one State into another, was, on motion of Mr. Randolph of

Virginia, stricken out, and " service" unanimously inserted, " the former being thought to express the condition of slaves, and the latter the obligation of free persons."

That such was the general understanding of the people will be the more manifest if we extend our examination beyond the Constitution as originally adopted, to the amendments subsequently incorporated into it. One of these amendments, as originally proposed by Virginia, provided that " no *freeman* should be deprived of life, liberty, or property, but *by the law of the land*," and was copied, substantially, from the English Magna Charta. Congress altered the phraseology by inserting, in lieu of the words quoted, " no PERSON shall be deprived of life, liberty, or property, WITHOUT DUE PROCESS OF LAW ;" and, thus altered, the proposed amendment became part of the Constitution. We are aware that it has been held by distinguished authority, that the section of the amended Constitution, which contains this provision, operates as a limitation only on national and not upon State legislation. Without controverting this opinion here, it is enough to say that, at the least, the clause prohibits the General Government from sanctioning slaveholding, and renders the continuance of slavery, as a legal relation, in any place of exclusive national jurisdiction, impossible.

For, what is slavery ?*   It is the complete and

---

* See Note 2 in Appendix.

absolute subjection of one person to the control and disposal of another person, by legalized force. We need not argue that no person can be, *rightfully,* compelled to submit to such control and disposal. All such subjection must originate in force; and, private force not being strong enough to accomplish the purpose, public force, in the form of law, must lend its aid. The Government comes to the help of the individual slaveholder, and punishes resistance to his will, and compels submission. THE GOVERNMENT, *therefore, in the case of every individual slave, is* THE REAL ENSLAVER, depriving each person enslaved of all liberty and all property, and all that makes life dear, without imputation of crime or any legal process whatsoever. This is precisely what the Government of the United States is forbidden to do by the Constitution. The Government of the United States, therefore, cannot create or continue the relation of master and slave. Nor can that relation be created or continued in any place, district, or territory, over which the jurisdiction of the National Government is exclusive; for slavery cannot subsist a moment after the support of the public force has been withdrawn.

We need not go further to prove that slaveholding in the States can have no rightful sanction or support from national authority, but must depend wholly upon State law for existence and continuance.

We have thus proved, from the Public Acts of the Nation, that, up to the time of the adoption of the Constitution, the people of the United States were an anti-slavery people; that the sanction of the national approbation was never given, and never intended to be given, to slaveholding; that, on the contrary, the Government of the United States was expressly forbidden to deprive any person of liberty, without due legal process; and that the policy of excluding slavery from all national territory, and restricting it within the limits of the original States, was early adopted and practically applied.

SENTIMENTS OF DISTINGUISHED MEN OF THE REVOLUTIONARY PERIOD.

Permit us now, fellow citizens, to call your attention to the recorded opinions of the Patriots and Sages of the Revolutionary Era; from which you will learn that many of them, so far from desiring that the General Government should sanction slavery or extend its limits, were displeased that it was not, in terms, empowered to take action for its final extinction in the States, and that almost all looked forward to its final removal by State authority with expectation and hope.

The Preamble of the Abolition Act of Pennsylvania of 1780, exhibits clearly the state of many minds. "Weaned," says the General Assembly, "by a long course of experience from those narrow prejudices and partialities we had imbibed, we find our hearts enlarged with kindness and benevolence towards men of all conditions and nations; and we conceive ourselves, at this particular period, extraordinarily called upon by the blessing we have received, to manifest the sincerity of our professions and to give a substantial proof of our gratitude."

The sentiments of Mr. Jefferson are too well known to justify large quotations from his writings. We invite, however, your attention to two sentences; and will observe, in passing, that his opinions were shared by almost every Virginian of distinguished patriotism or ability.

In his Notes on Virginia, he said: "I think a change already perceptible since the origin of the present revolution. The spirit of the master is abating, that of the slave is rising from the dust, his condition mollifying, the way, I hope, preparing, under the auspices of Heaven, for a total emancipation; and that is disposed, in the order of events, to be with the consent of the masters, rather than by their extirpation."

On another occasion he said: "Nobody wishes more ardently than I to see an abolition not only of the trade, but of the condition of slavery; and certainly nobody will be more willing to encounter every sacrifice for that object."

In a letter to John F. Mercer, George Washington said: "I never mean, unless some particular circumstances should compel me to it, to possess another slave by purchase; it being among my first wishes to see some plan adopted by which slavery in this country may be abolished by law."

In a letter to Sir John Sinclair, assigning reasons for the depreciation of Southern lands, he said : " There are in Pennsylvania laws for the gradual abolition of slavery, which neither Virginia nor Maryland have at present, but which nothing is more certain than that they must have, and at a period not remote." *

General Lee of Virginia, in his " Memoirs on the Revolutionary War," remarked, " The Constitution of the United States, adopted lately with so much difficulty, has effectually provided against this evil, (the slave-trade,) after a few years. It is much to be lamented, that, having done so much in this way, a provision had not been made for the gradual abolition of slavery."

Judge Tucker, of Virginia, in a letter to the General Assembly of that State, in 1796, recommending the abolition of slavery, and speaking of the slaves in Virginia, said : " Should we not at the time of the Revolution have loosed their chains and broken their fetters ? or, if the difficulties and dangers of such an experiment prohibited the attempt during the convulsions of a revolution, is it not our duty to embrace the first moment of constitutional health and vigour to effectuate so desirable an

---

* See Note 3 in Appendix.

object, and to remove from us a stigma with which our enemies will never fail to upbraid us, nor our consciences to reproach us ? "

Luther Martin, of Maryland, left the Convention before the Constitution was finally completed. He opposed its adoption, and assigned, in his report to the Maryland legislature, as a leading reason for his opposition, the absence from the instrument of express provisions against slavery. He said that it was urged in the Convention, " that by the proposed system we were giving the General Government full and absolute power to regulate commerce, under which general power it would have a right to restrain or totally prohibit the slave-trade ; it must, therefore, appear to the world absurd and disgraceful to the last degree, that we should except from the exercise of that power the only branch of commerce which is unjustifiable in its nature, and contrary to the rights of mankind :—that, on the contrary, we ought rather to prohibit expressly in our Constitution the further importation of slaves, and to authorize the General Government, from time to time, to make such regulations as should be thought most advantageous for the gradual abolition of slavery, and the emancipation of the slaves which are already in the States."

James Wilson, of Pennsylvania, signed the Constitution, taking a very different view of its provisions, bearing upon slavery, from that of Mr. Martin, but agreeing with him entirely as to slavery itself. In the Ratification Convention of Pennsylvania, speaking of the clause relating to the power of Congress over the slave-trade after twenty years, he said: " I consider this clause as laying the foundation for banishing slavery out of this country. It will produce the same kind of gradual change which was produced in Pennsylvania: the NEW STATES, which are to be formed, will be under the control of Congress in this particular, and SLAVERY WILL NEVER BE INTRODUCED AMONG THEM. It presents us with the pleasing prospect that the rights of mankind will be acknowledged and established throughout the Union."

In the Ratification Convention of Massachusetts, Gen. Heath declared that " Slavery was CONFINED TO THE STATES NOW EXISTING: *it could not be extended.* By their ordinance Congress had declared that THE NEW STATES should be republican, and *have no slavery.*"*

In the Ratification Convention of North Carolina, Mr. Iredell, afterwards a Justice of the Supreme Court of the United States, observed, " When the entire abolition of slavery takes place, it will be an event which must be pleasing to every generous mind and every friend of human nature."

In the Ratification Convention of Virginia, Mr. Johnson said, " The principle of emancipation has

---

* See Note 4 in Appendix.

begun since the revolution. Let us do what we will, it will come round."

In the course of the debate in the Congress of 1789, the first under the Constitution, on a petition against the slave-trade, Mr. Parker, of Virginia, remarked, that "he hoped Congress would do all that lay in their power to restore human nature to its inherent privileges, and, if possible, wipe off the stigma which America laboured under. The inconsistency in our principles, with which we are justly charged, should be done away, that we may show by our actions the pure beneficence of the doctrine which we held out to the world in our Declaration of Independence." In the same debate Mr. Brown, of North Carolina, observed, "The emancipation of the slaves will be effected in time: it ought to be a gradual business; but he hoped *Congress would not precipitate it* to the great injury of the Southern States." And Mr. Jackson, of Georgia, complained, "That it was THE FASHION OF THE DAY to favour the liberty of the slaves."

These citations might be indefinitely multiplied, but we forbear. Well might Mr. Leigh, of Virginia, remark, in 1832, "I thought, till very lately, that IT WAS KNOWN TO EVERYBODY, that during the revolution, and for many years after, *the abolition of slavery was a favourite topic with many of our ablest statesmen*, who entertained, with respect, all the schemes which wisdom or ingenuity could suggest for accomplishing the object."

Fellow Citizens: The public acts, and the recorded opinions of the fathers of the revolution are before you. Let us pause here. Let us reflect what would have been the condition of the country had the original policy of the nation been steadily pursued, and contrast what would have been with what is.

At the time of the adoption of the Constitution, Massachusetts, Rhode Island, Connecticut, New Hampshire, and Pennsylvania, had become non-slaveholding States. By the ordinance of 1787, provision had been made for the erection of five other non-slaveholding States. The admission of Vermont and the District of Maine, as separate States, without slavery, was also anticipated. There was no doubt that New York and New Jersey would follow the example of Pennsylvania. Thus it was supposed to be certain that the Union would ultimately embrace at least fourteen Free states, and that slavery would be excluded from all territory thereafter acquired by the nation, and from all States created out of such territory.

This was the true understanding upon which the Constitution was adopted. It was never imagined that new Slave states were to be admitted; unless,

perhaps, which seems probable, it was contemplated
to admit the western districts of Virginia and North
Carolina, now known as Kentucky and Tennessee,
as States, without any reference to the slavery
already established in them. In no event, to which
our fathers look forward, could the number of Slave
states exceed eight, while it was almost certain
that the number of Free states would be at least
fourteen. It was never supposed that slavery was
to be a cherished interest of the country, or even a
permanent institution of any State. It was expected
that all the States, stimulated by the examples
before them, and urged by their own avowed principles recorded in the Declaration, would, at no
distant day, put an end to slavery within their
respective limits. So strong was this expectation,
that JAMES CAMPBELL, in an address at Philadelphia, before the Society of the Cincinnati, in
1787, which was attended by the Constitution
Convention, then in session, declared, " The time is
not far distant when our sister States, in imitation
of our example, shall turn their vassals into freemen." And Jonathan Edwards predicted in 1791,
that, in fifty years from this time, it will be as disgraceful for a man to hold a negro slave, as to be
guilty of common robbery or theft.

It cannot be doubted that, had the original policy
and original principles of the Government been
adhered to, this expectation would have been
realized. The example and influence of the

General Government would have been on the side of freedom. Slavery would have ceased in the District of Columbia immediately upon the establishment of the Government within its limits. Slavery would have disappeared from Louisiana and Florida upon the acquisition of those territories by the United States. No laws would have been enacted, no treaties made, no measures taken for the extension or maintenance of slavery. Amid the rejoicings of all the free, and the congratulations of all friends of freedom, the last fetter would, ere now, have been stricken from the last slave, and the principles and institutions of liberty would have pervaded the entire land.

ACTUAL RESULTS.

How different—how sadly different are the facts of history! Luther Martin complained, at the time of the adoption of the Constitution, " that when our own liberties were at stake, we warmly felt for the common rights of men: the danger being thought to be passed which threatened ourselves, we are daily growing more and more insensible to those rights." This insensibility continued to increase, and prepared the way for the encroachments of the political Slave power, which originated in the three-fifths rule of the Constitution. This rule, designed, perhaps, as a censure upon slavery, by denying to the Slave states the full representation to which their population would entitle them,

has had a very different practical effect. It has
virtually established in the country an aristocracy
of slaveholders. It has conferred on masters the
right of representation for three-fifths of their slaves.
The representation from the Slave states in Congress has always been from one-fifth to one-fourth
greater than it would have been, were freemen
only represented.* Under the first apportionment,
according to this rate, a district in a Free state,
containing thirty thousand free inhabitants, would
have one representative. A district in a Slave
state, containing three thousand free persons and
forty-five thousand slaves, would also have one.
In the first district a representative could be elected
only by the majority of five thousand votes : in
the other, he would need only the majority of five
hundred. Of course, the representation from Slave
states, elected by a much smaller constituency, and
bound together by a common tie, would generally
act in concert, and always with special regard to
the interests of masters whose representatives in
fact they were. Every aristocracy in the world has
sustained itself by encroachment, and the aristocracy
of slaveholders in this country has not been an
exception to the general truth. The nation has
always been divided into parties, and the slaveholders, by making the protection and advancement
of their peculiar interests the price of their political

---

* See note 5 in Appendix.

G

support, have generally succeeded in controlling
all. This influence has greatly increased the insensibility to human rights, of which MARTIN in-
dignantly complained. It has upheld slavery in
the District of Columbia and in the Territories, in
spite of the Constitution : it has added to the Union
six Slave states created out of national Territories :*
it has usurped the control of our foreign negotia-
tion,† and domestic legislation : ‡ it has dictated
the choice of the high offices of our Government
at home,§ and of our national representatives
abroad : ‖ it has filled every department of executive and judicial administration with its friends and
satellites : ¶ it has detained in slavery multitudes
who are constitutionally entitled to their freedom :
it has waged unrelenting war with the most sacred
rights of the free, stifling the freedom of speeches
and of debate, setting at naught the right of petition,
and denying in the Slave states those immunities
to the citizens of the free, which the Constitution
guarantees : and, finally, it has dictated the
acquisition of an immense foreign territory, not for
the laudable purpose of extending the blessings of
freedom, but with the bad design of diffusing the

---

* See note 6 in Appendix.
† See note 7 in Appendix.
‡ See note 8 in Appendix.
§ See note 9 in Appendix.
‖ See note 10 in Appendix.
¶ See note 11 in Appendix.

curse of slavery, and thereby consolidating and perpetuating its own ascendancy.

WHAT WE MEAN TO DO.

AGAINST this influence, against these infractions of the Constitution, against these departures from the national policy originally adopted, against these violations of the national faith originally pledged, we solemnly protest. Nor do we propose only to protest. We recognize the obligations which rest upon us as descendants of the men of the revolution, as inheritors of the institutions which they established, as partakers of the blessings which they so dearly purchased, to carry forward and perfect their work. We mean to do it, wisely and prudently, but with energy and decision. We have the example of our fathers on our side. We have the Constitution of their adoption on our side. It is our duty, and our purpose, to rescue the Government from the control of the slaveholders; to harmonize its practical administration with the provisions of the Constitution, and to secure to all, without exception, and without partiality, the rights which the Constitution guarantees. We believe that slaveholding, in the United States, is the source of numberless evils, moral, social, and political; that it hinders social progress; that it embitters public and private intercourse; that it degrades us as individuals, as States, and as a nation; that it holds back our country from a splendid career of greatness and glory. We are, therefore, resolutely, inflexibly, at all times, and under all circumstances, hostile to its longer continuance in our land. We believe that its removal can be effected peacefully, constitutionally, without real injury to any, with the greatest benefit to all.

HOW WE MEAN TO DO IT.

WE propose to effect this by repealing all legislation, and discontinuing all action, in favor of slavery, at home and abroad; by prohibiting the practice of slaveholding in all places of exclusive national jurisdiction, in the District of Columbia, in American vessels upon the seas, in forts, arsenals, navy yards; by forbidding the employment of slaves upon any public work; by adopting resolutions in Congress, declaring that slaveholding, in all States created out of national territories, is unconstitutional, and recommending to the others the immediate adoption of measures for its extinction within their respective limits; and by electing and appointing to public station such men, and only such men as openly avow our principles, and will honestly carry out our measures.

The constitutionality of this line of action cannot be successfully impeached. That it will terminate, if steadily pursued, in the utter overthrow of slavery at no very distant day none will doubt. We adopt it, because we desire, through, and by the Constitution, to attain the great ends which the

Constitution itself proposes, the establishment of justice, and the security of liberty. We insist not, here, upon the opinions of some, that no slave-holding, in any State of the Union, is compatible with a true and just construction of the Constitution; nor upon the opinions of others, that the Declaration of Independence, setting forth the creed of the nation, that all men are created equal, and endowed by their Creator with an inalienable right of liberty, must be regarded as the common law of America, antecedent to, and unimpaired by the Constitution; nor need we appeal to the doctrine that slaveholding is contrary to the supreme law of the Supreme Ruler, preceding and controlling all human law, and binding upon all legislatures in the enactment of laws, and upon all courts in the administration of justice. We are willing to take our stand upon propositions generally conceded :—that slaveholding is contrary to natural right and justice; that it can subsist nowhere without the sanction and aid of positive legislation; that the Constitution expressly prohibits Congress from depriving any person of liberty without due process of law. From these propositions we deduce, by logical inference, the doctrines upon which we insist. We deprecate all discord among the States; but do not dread discord so much as we do the subjugation of the States and the people to the yoke of the slave-holding oligarchy. We deprecate the dissolution of the Union as a dreadful political calamity; but if any of the States shall prefer dissolution to submission to the Constitutional action of the people on the subject of slavery, we cannot purchase their alliance by the sacrifice of inestimable rights, and the abandonment of sacred duties.

Such, fellow citizens, are our views, principles, and objects.* We invite your co-operation in the great work of delivering our beloved country from the evils of slavery. No question half so important as that of slavery engages the attention of the American people. All others, in fact, dwindle into insignificance in comparison with it. The question of slavery is, and, until it shall be settled, must be, the paramount moral and political question of the day. We, at least, so regard it; and, so regarding it, must subordinate every other question to it.

It follows, as a necessary consequence, that we cannot yield our political support to any party which does not take our ground upon this question.

THE DIFFERENT PARTIES.

I. *The Democratic Party.*

WHAT, then, is the position of the political parties of the country in relation to this subject? One of these parties professes to be guided by the most liberal principles. "Equal and exact justice to all men;" "equal rights for all men;" "inflexible

---

* See note 12 in Appendix.

opposition to oppression," are its favourite mottoes.
It claims to be the true friend of popular government, and assumes the name of Democratic.
Among its members are, doubtless, many who
cherish its professions as sacred principles, and
believe that great cause of Freedom and Progress
is to be served by promoting its ascendancy. But
when we compare the maxims of the so-called
Democratic party with its acts, its hypocrisy is
plainly revealed. Among its leading members we
find the principal slaveholders the chiefs of the
oligarchy. It has never scrupled to sacrifice the
rights of the Free states, or of the people, to the
demands of the Slave power. Like Sir Pertinax
McSycophant, its northern leaders believe that the
great secret of advancement lies in " bowing well."
No servility seems too gross, no self-degradation
too great, to be submitted to.* They think themselves well rewarded, if the unity of the party be
preserved, and the spoils of victory secured. If,
in the distribution of these spoils, they receive only
the jackall's share, they content themselves with
the reflection that little is better than nothing.
They declaim loudly against all monopolies, all
special privileges, all encroachments on personal
rights, all distinctions founded upon birth, and
compensate themselves for these efforts of virtue,
by practising the vilest oppression upon all their

* See note 13 in Appendix.

countrymen, in whose complexions the slightest trace of African derivation can be detected.

Profoundly do we revere the maxims of true Democracy; they are identical with those of true Christianity, in relation to the rights and duties of men as citizens. And our reverence for Democratic principles is the precise measure of our detestation of the policy of those who are permitted to shape the action of the Democratic party. Political concert with that party, under its present leadership, is, therefore, plainly impossible. Nor do we entertain the hope, which many, no doubt, honestly cherish, that the professed principles of the party will, at length, bring it right upon the question of slavery. Its professed principles have been the same for nearly half a century, and yet the subjection of the party to the Slave power is, at this moment, as complete as ever. There is no prospect of any change for the better, until those democrats whose hearts are really possessed by a generous love of liberty for all, and by an honest hatred of oppression, shall manfully assert their individual independence, and refuse their support to the panders of slavery.

2. *The Whig Party.*

There is another party which boasts that it is conservative in its character. Its watchwords are "a tariff," "a banking system," "the Union as it is." Among its members, also, are many sincere

opponents of slavery; and the party itself, seeking
aid in the attainment of power, and anxious to
carry its favorite measures, and bound together by
no such professed principles as secure the unity of
the Democratic party, often concedes much to
their anti-slavery views. It is not unwilling, in
those States and parts of States where anti-slavery
sentiment prevails, to assume an anti-slavery atti-
tude, and claim to be an anti-slavery party. Like
the Democratic party, however, the Whig party
maintains alliances with the slaveholders. It proposes, in its national conventions, no action against
slavery. It has no anti-slavery article in its
national creed. Among its leaders and champions
in Congress, and out of Congress, none are so
honored and trusted as slaveholders in practice and
in principle. Whatever the Whig party, therefore,
concedes to anti-slavery, must be reluctantly conceded. Its natural position is conservative. Its
natural line of action is to maintain things as they
are. Its natural bond of union is regard for
interests rather than for rights. There are,
doubtless, zealous opponents of slavery, who are
also zealous Whigs; but they have not the general
confidence of their party; they are under the ban
of the slaveholders; and in any practical anti-
slavery movement, as, for example, the repeal of
the laws which sanction slaveholding in the District of Columbia, would meet the determined
opposition of a large and most influential section

of the party, not because the people of the Free states would be opposed to the measure, but because it would be displeasing to the oligarchy and fatal to party unity. We are constrained to think, therefore, that all expectation of efficient anti-slavery action from the Whig party, as now organized, will prove delusive. Nor do we perceive any probability of a change in its organization, separating its anti-slavery from its pro-slavery constituents, and leaving the former in possession of the name and influence of the party. With the Whig party, therefore, as at present organized, it is as impossible for us, whose mottoes are " Equal Rights and Fair Wages for all," and " the Union as it should be," to act in alliance and concert, as it is for us so to act with the so-called Democratic party. We cannot choose between these parties for the sake of any local or partial advantage, without sacrificing consistency, self-respect, and mutual confidence. While we say this, we are bound to add, that were either of these parties to disappoint our expectations, and to adopt into its *national creed as its leading articles*, the principles which we regard as fundamental, and enter upon a course of unfeigned and earnest action against the system of slavery, we should not hesitate, regarding, as we do, the question of slavery as the paramount question of our day and nation, to give to it our cordial and vigorous support, until slavery should be no more.

With what party, then, shall we aci? Or shall we act with none? Act, in some way, we must: for the possession of the right of suffrage, the right of electing our own law-makers and rulers, imposes upon us the corresponding duty of voting for men who will carry out the views which we deem of paramount importance and obligation. Act together we must; for upon the questions which we regard as the most vital we are fully agreed. We must act then; act together; and act against slavery and oppression. Acting thus, we necessarily act as a party; for what is a party, but a body of citizens, acting together politically, in good faith, upon common principles, for a common object? And if there be a party already in existence, animated by the same motives, and aiming at the same results as ourselves, we must act with and in that party.

THE LIBERTY PARTY.

That there is such a party is well known. It is the Liberty party of the United States. Its principles, measures, and objects we cordially approve. It founds itself upon the great cardinal principle of true Democracy and of true Christianity, the brotherhood of the Human Family. It avows its purpose to wage implacable war against slaveholding as the direst form of oppression, and then against every other species of tyranny and injustice. Its views on the subject of slavery in this country are, in the main, the same as those which we have set

forth in this address. Its members agree to regard
the extinction of slavery as the most important end
which can, at this time, be proposed to political
action ; and they agree to differ as to other questions of minor importance, such as those of trade
and currency, believing that these can be satisfactorily disposed of, when the question of slavery
shall be settled, and that, until then, they cannot
be satisfactorily disposed of at all.

The rise of such a party as this was anticipated
long before its actual organization, by the single-
hearted and patriotic Charles Follen, a German by
birth, but a true American by adoption and in
spirit. " If there ever is to be in this country," he
said in 1836, " a party that shall take its name and
character, not from particular liberal measures or
popular men, but from its uncompromising and
consistent adherence to freedom---a truly liberal
and thoroughly republican party, it must direct its
first decided effort against the grossest form, the
most complete manifestation of oppression ; and,
having taken anti-slavery ground, it must carry out
the principle of Liberty in all its consequences. It
must support every measure conducive to the
greatest possible individual and social, moral, intellectual, religious, and political freedom, whether
that measure be brought forward by inconsistent
slaveholders or consistent freemen. It must embrace the whole sphere of human action ; watching
and opposing the slightest illiberal and anti-repub-

lican tendency, and concentrating its whole force and influence against slavery itself, in comparison with which every other species of tyranny is tolerable, and by which every other is strengthened and justified."

Thus wrote Charles Follen in 1836. It is impossible to express better the want which enlightened lovers of liberty felt of a real Democratic party in the country—Democratic not in name only, but in deed and in truth. In this want, thus felt, the Liberty party had its origin,* and so long as this want remains otherwise unsatisfied, the Liberty party must exist; not as a mere Abolition party, but as a truly Democratic party, which aims at the extinction of slavery, because slaveholding is inconsistent with Democratic principles; aims at it, not as an ultimate end, but as the most important present object; as a great and necessary step in the work of reform; as an illustrious era in the advancement of society, to be wrought out by its action and instrumentality. The Liberty party of 1845 is, in truth, the Liberty party of 1776 revived. It is more: It is the party of Advancement and Freedom, which has, in every age, and with varying success, fought the battles of Human Liberty, against the party of False Conservatism and Slavery.

---

* See Note 14 in Appendix.

WILL YOU NOT JOIN IT?

AND now, fellow citizens, permit us to ask, whether you will not give to this party the aid of your votes, and of your counsels? Its aims are lofty, and noble, and pacific; its means are simple and unobjectionable. Why should it not have your co-operation?

ANTI-SLAVERY MEN!

ARE you already anti-slavery men? Let us ask, is it not far better to act with those with whom you agree on the fundamental point of slavery, and swell the vote and augment the moral force of anti-slavery, rather than to act with those with whom you agree only on minor points; and thus, for the time, swell a vote and augment an influence which must be counted against the Liberty movement, in the vain hope that those with whom you thus act now, will, at some indefinite future period, act with you for the overthrow of slavery? There are, perhaps, nearly equal numbers of you in each of the pro-slavery parties, honestly opposed to each other on questions of trade, currency, and extension of territory, but of one mind on the great question of slavery; and yet you suffer yourselves to be played off against each other by parties which agree in nothing except hostility to the great measure of positive action against slavery, which seems to you, and is, of paramount importance. What can you gain by this course? What may you not gain by laying your minor difference on the altar of duty, and uniting as one man, in one party, against slavery? Then every vote would tell for freedom, and would encourage the friends of liberty to fresh efforts. Now every vote, whether you intend it so or not, tells for slavery, and operates as a discouragement and hindrance to those who are contending for equal rights. Let us entreat you not to persevere in your suicidal, fratricidal course; but to renounce at once all pro-slavery alliances, and join the friends of liberty. It is not the question now whether a Liberty party shall be organized; it is organized and in the field. The real question, and the only real question, is: Will you, so far as your votes and influence go, hasten or retard the day of its triumph?

ALL MEN OF THE FREE STATES!

ARE you men of the Free states? And have you not suffered enough of wrong, of insult, and of contumely, from the slaveholding oligarchy?[*] Have you not been taxed enough for the support of slavery?[†] Is it not enough that all the powers of the government are exerted for its maintenance,[‡] and that all the Departments of the Government are in the hands of the Slave power? How long

---

[*] See Note 15 in Appendix.
[†] See Note 16 in Appendix.
[‡] See Note 17 in Appendix.

will you consent by your votes to maintain slavery
at the seat of the National Government, in violation of the Constitution of your country, and thus
give your direct sanction to the whole dreadful
system ?   How long will you consent to be represented in the National Councils by men who will
not dare to assert their own rights or yours in the
presence of an arrogant aristocracy; and, in your
State Legislatures, by men whose utmost height of
courage and manly daring, when your citizens are
imprisoned, without allegation of crime, in Slave
states, and your agents, sent for their relief, are
driven out, as you would scourge from your pre-
mises an intrusive cur, is to PROTEST *and submit?*
Rouse up, men of the Free states, for shame, if
not for duty !   Awake to a sense of your degraded
position.   Behold your President, a slaveholder;
his cabinet composed of slaveholders or their abject
instruments; the two Houses of Congress submis-
sive and servile; your representatives with foreign
nations, most of them slaveholders; your supreme
administrators of justice, most of them slaveholders;
your officers of the army and navy, most of them
slaveholders.*   Observe the results.   What numerous appointments of pro-slavery citizens of Slave
states to national employments ! What careful
exclusion of every man who holds the faith of
Jefferson and Washington in respect to slavery,

---

* See Note 13 in Appendix.

and believes with Madison " that it is wrong to admit in the Constitution the idea of property in man," from national offices of honor and trust! *
What assiduity in negotiations for the reclamation of slaves, cast, in the Providence of God, on foreign shores,† and for the extension of the markets of cotton, and rice, and tobacco, ay, and of men! What zeal on the judicial bench in wresting the Constitution and the law to the purposes of slave-holders, by shielding kidnappers from merited punishment, and paralyzing State legislation for the security of personal liberty! What readiness in legislation to serve the interests of the oligarchy by unconstitutional provisions for the recovery of fugitive slaves, and by laying heavy duties on slave-labor products, thereby compelling non-slaveholding laborers to support slaveholders in idleness and luxury! When shall these things have an end? How long shall servile endurance be protracted? It is for you, fellow citizens, to determine. The shameful partiality to slaveholders and slavery which has so long prevailed, and now prevails, in the administration of the government, will cease when you determine that it shall cease, and act accordingly.

---

* See Note 19 in Appendix.
† See Note 20 in Appendix.

ALL NON-SLAVEHOLDERS OF THE SLAVE STATES !

ARE you non-slaveholders of the Slave states? Let us ask you to consider what interest you have in the system of slavery. What benefits does it confer on you? What blessings does it promise to your children? You constitute the vast majority of the population of the Slave states. The aggregate votes of all the slaveholders do not exceed one hundred and fifty thousand, while the votes of the non-slaveholders are at least six hundred thousand, supposing each adult male to possess a vote. It is clear, therefore, that the continuance of slavery depends upon your suffrages. We repeat, what interest have you in supporting the system?

THE FRUITS OF SLAVERY.

SLAVERY diminishes your population and hinders your prosperity. Compare New York with Virginia, Ohio with Kentucky, Arkansas with Michigan, Florida with Iowa. Need we say more? *

It prevents general education. It is not the interest of slaveholders that poor non-slaveholders should be educated. The census of 1840 reveals the astounding facts that more than one-seventeenth

---

* See Note 21 in Appendix.

of the white population in the Slave states are unable to read or write, while not a hundred and fiftieth part of the same class in the Free are in the same condition, and that there are more than twelve times as many scholars at public charge in the Free states as in the Slave states.*

It paralyzes your industry and enterprise. The census of 1840 also disclosed the fact that the Free states, with two millions and a quarter inhabitants more, and ninety-eight millions acres less than the Slave states, produce annually, in value, from mines, thirty-three millions dollars more; from the forests, eight millions dollars more; from fisheries, nine millions dollars more; from agriculture, forty millions dollars more; from manufactures, one hundred and fifty-one millions dollars more. At the same time, the capital invested in commerce by the Free states exceeds the capital similarly invested in the Slave states by more than one hundred millions of dollars; and the tonnage of the former exceeds the tonnage of the latter by more than a thousand millions tons! This enormous disparity, which will strike attention the more forcibly when it is considered that much of the capital employed in the Slave states is owned in the Free, can be ascribed to no cause except slavery.†

---

* See Note 22 in Appendix.
† See Note 23 in Appendix.

It degrades and dishonors labor. In what country did an aristocracy ever care for the poor? When did slaveholders ever attempt to improve the condition of the free laborer? "White negroes" is the contemptuous term by which Robert Wickliffe, of Kentucky, designated the free laborers of his State. He saw no distinction between them and slaves, except that the former may be converted into voters. Chancellor Harper, of South Carolina, teaches that, "so far as the mere laborer has the pride, the knowledge or the aspiration of a freeman, he is unfitted for his situation." And he likens the laborer "to the horse or the ox," to whom it would be ridiculous to attempt to impart "a cultivated understanding or fine feeling." Governor McDuffie, in a message to the legislature of South Carolina, went so far as to say that " the institution of domestic slavery supersedes the necessity of an order of nobility, and the other appendages of an hereditary system of government." Of course the slaveholders are the noble, and you, the non-slaveholders, are the ignoble, of this social system.

Slavery corrupts the religion and destroys the morals of a community. We need not repeat Jefferson's strong testimony. In a message to the legislature of Kentucky, some years since, the Governor said, "We long to see the day when the law will assert its majesty, and stop the wanton destruction of life which almost daily occurs within

the jurisdiction of this Commonwealth." And the
Governor of Alabama, in a message to the legislature of that State, said, " Why do we hear of stab-
bings and shootings, almost daily, in some part or
other of our State ? " A Judge in New Orleans,
in an address on the opening of his court, observed,
" Without some powerful and certain remedy our
streets will become butcheries, overflowing with the
blood of our citizens." These terrible pictures are
drawn by home pencils. Can communities prosper
when religion and morality furnish no stronger
restraints on violence and passion ?*

Slavery is a source of most deplorable weakness.
What a panic is spread by the bare suggestion of a
servile insurrection ! And how completely are the
slaveholding States at the mercy of any invading
foe who will raise the standard of emancipation !
In the revolutionary war, according to the secret
journals of Congress, South Carolina was " unable
to make any effectual efforts with militia, by reason
of the great proportion of citizens necessary to
remain at home to prevent insurrection among the
negroes, and to prevent the desertion of them to the
enemy." We need not say that if the danger of
insurrection was then great, it would be, circumstances being similar, tenfold greater now.†

---

* See Note 24 in Appendix.
† See Note 25 in Appendix.

Slavery seeks to deprive non-slaveholders of
political power. In Virginia and South Carolina
especially, has this policy been most steadily and
successfully pursued. In South Carolina the
political power of the State is lodged in the great
slaveholding districts by the Constitution, and to
make assurance doubly sure, it is provided, in that
instrument, that no person can be a member of the
legislature unless he owns five hundred acres of
land and ten slaves, or an equivalent in additional
land. The right of voting for electors of President
and Vice-President is, in South Carolina, confined
to members of the legislature; consequently, in
that State no non-slaveholder can have a voice in
the selection of the first and second officers of the
Republic. In Virginia the slave population is
considered the basis of political power, and the
preponderance of representation is given to those
districts in which there is the largest slave population. The House of Representatives consists of
one hundred and thirty-four members, of whom
fifty-six are chosen by the counties west of the
Blue Ridge, and seventy-eight by the counties
east. The Senate consists of thirty-two members,
of whom thirteen are assigned to the western, and
nineteen to the eastern counties. Already the free
white population west of the Blue Ridge exceeds
the same class east in number, but no change in the
population can affect this distribution of political
power, designed to secure and preserve the ascen-

dancy of the slaveholders, who chiefly reside east of the Ridge, so long as the Constitution remains unchanged.

TO NON-SLAVEHOLDERS.

These, non-slaveholders of the Slave states, are the fruits of slavery. You surely can have no reason to love a system which entails such consequences. Yet it lives by your sufferance. You have only to speak the word at the ballot-box, and the system falls.* Will you be restrained from speaking that word by the consideration that the enslaved will be benefited as well as yourselves? or by the selfish expectation that you may yourselves become slaveholders hereafter, and so be admitted into the ranks of the aristocracy? If such considerations withhold you, we bid you beware lest you prepare a bitter retribution for yourselves, and find, to your mortification and shame, that a patent of nobility, written in the tears and blood of the oppressed, is a sorry passport to the approbation of mankind.

TO SLAVEHOLDERS.

We would appeal, also, to slaveholders themselves. We would enter at once within the lines of selfish ideas and mercenary motives, and appeal to your consciences and your hearts. You know that the

---

* See Note 26 in Appendix.

system of slaveholding is wrong. Whatever theologians may teach and cite Scripture for, you know —all of you who claim freedom for yourselves and your children as a birthright precious beyond all price, and inalienable as life—that no person can rightfully hold another as a slave. Your courts, in their judicial decisions, and your books of common law in their elementary lessons, rise far above the precepts of most of your religious teachers, and declare all slaveholding to be against natural right. You feel it to be so. God has so made the human heart, that, in spite of all theological sophistry and pretended Scripture proofs, you cannot help feeling it to be so. There is a law of sublimer origin and more awful sanction than any human code, written, in effaceable characters, upon every heart of man, which binds all to do unto others as they would that others should do unto them. And where is there one of all your number who would exchange conditions with the happiest of all your slaves? Produce the man! And until he is produced, let theological apologists for slaveholding keep silence. Most earnestly would we entreat you to listen to the voice of conscience and obey the promptings of humanity. We are not your enemies. We do not pretend to any superior virtue; or that we, being in your circumstances, would be likely to act differently from you. But we are all fellow citizens of the same great Republic. We feel slaveholding to be a dreadful incubus upon us, dishonoring us in the eyes of foreign nations ; nullifying the force of our example of free institutions ; holding us back from a glorious career of prosperity and renown ; sowing broadcast the seeds of discord, division, disunion : and we are anxious for its extinction. With Jefferson, we tremble for our country, when we "remember that God is just, and that his justice cannot sleep for ever." With Washington, we believe "that there is but one proper and effectual mode by which the extinction of slavery can be accomplished, and that is, by legislative authority ; and this, so far as our suffrages will go, shall not be wanting."

We would not invade the Constitution ; but we would have the Constitution rightly construed and administered according to its true sense and spirit. We would not dictate the mode in which slavery shall be attacked in particular States ; but we would have it removed at once from all places under the exclusive jurisdiction of the National Government, and also, have immediate measures taken, in accordance with constitutional rights and the principles of justice, for its removal from each State by State authority. In this work we ask your co-operation. Shall we ask in vain ? Are you not convinced that the almost absolute monopoly of the offices and the patronage of the government, and the almost exclusive control of its legislation and executive and judicial administration, by slaveholders, and for the purposes of slavery, is unjust to the non-slaveholders of the country? * Can you blame us for saying that we will no longer sanction it? Are you not satisfied, to use the language of one of your own number, "that slavery is a cancer, a slow consuming cancer, a withering pestilence, an unmitigated curse?" And can you wonder that we should be anxious, by all just, and honorable, and constitutional means, to effect its extinction in our respective States, and to confine it to its constitutional limits? Are you not fully aware that the gross inconsistency of slaveholding with our professed principles astonishes the world, and makes the name of our country a mock, and the name of liberty a by-word? And can you regret that we should exert ourselves to the utmost to redeem our glorious land and her institutions from just reproach, and, by illustrious acts of mercy and justice, place ourselves, once more, in the van of Human Progress and Advancement?

TO ALL FRIENDS OF LIBERTY, AND OF OUR COUNTRY'S BEST INTERESTS.

FINALLY, we ask all true friends of liberty, of impartial, universal liberty, to be firm and steadfast. The little handful of voters, who, in 1840, wearied of compromising expediency, and despair-

---

* See Note 27 in Appendix.

ing of anti-slavery action by pro-slavery parties, raised anew the standard of the Declaration, and manfully resolved to vote right then and vote for freedom, has already swelled to a GREAT PARTY, strong enough, numerically, to decide the issue of any national contest, and stronger far in the power of its pure and elevating principles. And if these principles be sound, which we doubt not, and if the question of slavery be, as we verily believe it is, the GREAT QUESTION of our day and nation, it is a libel upon the intelligence, the patriotism, and the virtue of the American people to say that there is no hope that a majority will not array themselves under our banner. Let it not be said that we are factious or impracticable. We adhere to our views because we believe them to be sound, practicable, and vitally important. We have already said that we are ready to prove our devotion to our principles by co-operation with either of the other two great American Parties, which will openly and honestly, in State and National Conventions, avow our doctrines and adopt our measures, until slavery shall be overthrown. We do not, indeed, expect any such adoption and avowal by either of those parties, because we are well aware that they fear more, at present, from the loss of slaveholding support than from the loss of anti-slavery co-operation. But we can be satisfied with nothing less, for we will compromise no longer; and, therefore, must of necessity maintain our separate organization as the true Democratic Party of the country, and trust our cause to the patronage of the people and the blessing of God!

Carry then, friends of freedom and free labor, your principles to the ballot-box. Let no difficulties discourage, no dangers daunt, no delays dishearten you. Your solemn vow that slavery must perish is registered in heaven. Renew that vow! Think of the martyrs of truth and freedom; think of the millions of the enslaved; think of the other millions of the oppressed and degraded free; and renew that vow! Be not tempted from the path of political duty. Vote for no man, act with no party politically connected with the supporters of slavery. Vote for no man, act with no party unwilling to adopt and carry out the principles which we have set forth in this address. To compromise for any partial or temporary advantage is ruin to our cause. To act with any party, or to vote for the candidates of any party, which recognizes the friends and supporters of slavery as members in full standing, because in particular places or under particular circumstances, it may make large professions of anti-slavery zeal, is to commit political suicide. Unswerving fidelity to our principles; unalterable determination to carry those principles to the ballot-box at every election; inflexible and unanimous support of those, and

only those, who are true to those principles, are
the conditions of our ultimate triumph. Let these
conditions be fulfilled, and our triumph is certain.
The indications of its coming multiply on every
hand. The clarion trump of freedom breaks
already the gloomy silence of slavery in Kentucky,
and its echoes are heard throughout the land. A
spirit of inquiry and of action is awakened everywhere. The assemblage of the convention, whose
voice we utter, is itself an auspicious omen.
Gathered from the North and the South, and the
East and West, we here unite our counsels, and
consolidate our action. We are resolved to go
forward, knowing that our cause is just, trusting
in God. We ask you to go forward with us,
invoking His blessing who sent His Son to redeem
mankind. With Him are the issues of all events.
He can and He will disappoint all the devices of
oppression. He can, and we trust He will, make
our instrumentality efficient for the redemption
of our land from slavery, and for the fulfilment of
our fathers' pledge in behalf of freedom, before
Him and before the world.*

---

* See Note 28 in Appendix.

APPENDIX.

CONSISTING OF NOTES TO THE

CINCINNATI ADDRESS.

APPENDIX.

HESE are precisely the same notes that were appended to the Cincinnati Address in 1845. But could similar notes, statistical and historical, be brought down to 1860, including accounts of the passage of the "Compromise Measures;" of the infamous "Fugitive Slave Law;" of the "lynchings" and murders of northern citizens in the Slave states; of the burnings of negroes; of the massacres of the peaceful settlers in Kansas, &c., &c., they would present a picture of horrible barbarities hardly paralleled on the page of history.

Note No. I.

The *Southern and Western Liberty Convention*, held at Cincinnati, on the 11th and 12th June, 1845, was the most remarkable Anti-Slavery body yet assembled in the United States. The call embraced all those who were resolved to act against Slavery, by speech, by the pen, by the press, and by the ballot. It was not therefore exclusively a Convention of the Liberty party; and accordingly not a few were in attendance who had not acted with that party. The whole number present, as

Delegates, was about two thousand—from the States of Ohio, Indiana, Illinois and Michigan; from the Territories of Wisconsin and Iowa; from Western Pennsylvania, and Western Virginia, and from Kentucky. Deputations were also present from Massachusetts, New York and Rhode Island; and the whole assembly, including spectators, varied during the sittings from two thousand five hundred, to four thousand persons. Letters were received from *Samuel Fessenden* and *Samuel H. Pond*, Me., *Titus Hutchinson*, Vt., *Elihu Burritt* and *H. B. Stanton*, and *Phineas Crandell*, Mass.; *Wm. Jay*, *Wm. H. Seward*, *Gerrit Smith*, *Horace Greeley*, *Wm. Goodell*, *Lewis Tappan*, New York; *C. D. Cleveland*, *F. Julius Lemoyne*, *Thomas Earle*, Pennsylvania; *F. D. Parish*, Ohio; *Cassius M. Clay*, Lexington, Ky., and *John Gilmore*, Virginia. The Chairman of the Committee which reported this able address, and by whom it was written, was *S. P. Chase*, Esq., of Cincinnati.

Note No. II.

"A slave is one who is in the power of his master, to whom he belongs. The master may sell him, dispose of his person, his industry, and his labor: he can do nothing, possess nothing, nor acquire anything but what must belong to his master."—*Law of Louisiana.*

" Slaves shall always be reputed and considered real estate; shall be, as such, subject to be mortgaged, according to the rules prescribed by law, and they shall be seized and sold as real estate."—*Law of Louisiana.*

" Penalty for any slave, or free colored person, exercising the functions of a minister of the gospel, THIRTY-NINE lashes." " Penalty for teaching a slave to read, imprisonment one year." " Every negro, or mulatto, found in the State, not able to show himself entitled to freedom, may be sold as a slave."—*Laws of Mississippi.*

" For attempting to teach any free colored person, or slave, to spell, read or write, a fine of not less than two hundred and fifty, nor more than five hundred dollars."—*Law of Alabama.*

" Any person who sees more than seven slaves without any white person, in a high road, may whip each slave twenty lashes." " Every colored person is presumed to be a slave, unless he can prove himself free." —*Laws of Georgia.*

" Slaves shall be deemed sold, taken, reputed, and adjudged, in law, to be chattels personal in the hands of their owners and possessors, and their executors, administrators, and assigns, TO ALL INTENTS, CONSTRUCTIONS, AND PURPOSES WHATEVER." " Whereas, many owners of slaves, and others, that have the management of them, do confine them so CLOSELY to hard labor, that they have not sufficient time for natural rest, be it enacted that no slave shall be compelled to labor more than FIFTEEN hours in the twenty-four, from March 25 to September 25, or FOURTEEN for the rest of the year." " Penalty for KILLING a slave in a sudden heat of passion, or by *undue correction*, a fine of five hundred dollars, and imprisonment *not over* six months!"—*Laws of South Carolina.*

" In the trial of slaves, the Sheriff chooses the Court,

which must consist of three Justices and twelve *slave-holders*, to serve as jurors."—*Law of Tennessee.*

"Any emancipated slave remaining in the State more than a year, may be sold by the *overseers of the poor*, for the benefit of the *literary* fund." "Any slave, or free colored person, found at any school for teaching reading or writing, by day or night, may be whipped, at the discretion of a Justice, not exceeding twenty lashes." "Any white person assembling with slaves, for the *purpose* of teaching them to read or write, shall be fined not less than ten, nor more than a hundred dollars."—*Laws of Virginia.* By the revised code of this State, SEVENTY-ONE offences are punished with DEATH, when committed by slaves, and by nothing more than imprisonment when by whites.

"Any slave convicted of petty treason, murder or wilful burning of dwelling-houses, may be sentenced to have the right hand cut off, to be hanged in the usual manner, the head severed from the body, the body divided into four quarters, and the head and quarters set up in the most public place in the county, where such fact was committed."—*Law of Maryland.*

We might extend such extracts from such laws, (if *laws* they can be called,) to the size of an octavo :— laws that would disgrace the most savage people upon the face of the earth. In reference to them, the editor of the New York Tribune, of November 25, 1845, thus speaks : " Laws which allow one man to sell another man a thousand miles away from his wife, and their children five hundred miles apart in other directions, without right or hope of reunion—which allow men to beat, ravish, or even murder women of the degraded

caste with impunity, in the presence of a dozen witnesses of their own color, if there are none of the
ruling caste to testify against them—laws, which give
to a white drunkard and gambler all the earnings of
an ingenious and industrious black family for life, with
privilege to flog them into the bargain—these *laws* are
hateful to God, and pernicious to mankind. We can
comprehend them as well in New York as in Kentucky,
and they cannot be less than infernal anywhere."

Note No. III.

In a letter to Robert Morris, Washington also said,
"There is only one proper and effectual mode by which
the abolition of slavery can be accomplished, and that is
by legislative authority; and this, as far as my suffrage
will go, shall never be wanting."

In a speech in the House of Delegates of Maryland,
Wm. Pinckney said, "By the eternal principles of
natural justice, no master in this State has a right to
hold his slave for a single hour."

Dr. Rush, of Pennsylvania, declared slavery to be
"repugnant to the principles of Christianity, and rebellion against the authority of a common Father."

Note No. IV.

In the same Convention, in reference to the provisions of the Constitution that Congress should have
power to stop the domestic slave trade, called in that
instrument " the migration of persons," Judge Dawes
remarked, that "slavery had received its death wound,
and would die of consumption."

Note No. V.

The whole number of representatives in the House is 223. Of these the Free states have 135, the Slave, 88; and of these 88, but 68 are the representatives of freemen, the remaining 20 being representatives of *slave property.*

The manner in which the present ratio of representation was fixed, is one which should cover with lasting disgrace the Northern representatives who voted for it. The number fixed by the House, was one representative for every 50,189 inhabitants. This would have given them 306 members; but the Senate, fearing the influence of so large a body of freemen as this would give, sent back the bill, with the ratio of 70,680, which would reduce the House to 223, and give the Free states a majority of 47, instead of 68. But why the odd number, 680? *It deprives four great States of the North, namely, Massachusetts, New York, Pennsylvania, and Ohio, of one member each.*

Even the correspondent of the New York Herald could thus write at the time: "The Senate apportionment has robbed the North of at least one quarter of its practical influence in the Union, when regarded in its full extent; and the members of the Free states who voted for it, have thus surrendered the rights of their constituents, and violated their trusts."

It is curious, also, to look at the fractions unrepresented. The Slave states have but 140,092; the Free, 218,678. The fraction of Virginia is but 2! that of Pennsylvania, 27,687.

In the Presidential contest of 1841, the Slave states

had 114 electors; the Free, 161; while the whole popular vote of the Slave states was but 693,434; the Free, 1,710,041. That is, while the Free states had but about two-fifths more in the number of electors, they had nearly three times as many popular votes. Pennsylvania had 26 electors, and a popular vote of 287,697; while Delaware, Maryland, and Virginia together, had 28 electors, and but 159,525 popular vote: that is, with but little more than half the popular vote they had two more electors.

Note No. VI.

Louisiana, Mississippi, Alabama, Missouri, Arkansas, and Florida.

Note No. VII.

It is well known that by far the greater number of our foreign ministers have been from the Slave states, and that they have ever been most vigilant to promote the interests of those States, while the far more important interests of the Free states have been, comparatively, neglected. In 1841, out of seven persons nominated, in succession, for diplomatic stations, six were from the Slave states, which were all immediately confirmed, while the nomination of the seventh, Edward Everett of Massachusetts, was laid on the table, till the slaveholders could satisfy themselves that he had no views adverse to their "peculiar institutions."

What untold benefit would it have been to our Free states, if foreign nations had been induced, as they doubtless might have been, to favor our agricultural and manufacturing products, as they have been induced, by slaveholding ministers, to favour COTTON, TOBACCO, AND RICE!

NOTE No. VIII.

No one man has so much influence over our "domestic legislation," as the Speaker of the House of Representatives. He it is that appoints all the committees, which committees bring before the House such subjects, and present them in such aspects, as best suit their views. Since the organization of our government, in 1789, out of the 56 years the Slave states have had the Speaker 38 years, the Free, 18 years. With the exception of John W. Taylor, of New York, who served three years, the Free states did not give a Speaker to the House from 1809 to 1845.

NOTE No. IX.

Of the TEN Presidents, since 1789, the Slave states have had SIX, who will have served at the end of the present term, 44 years; the Free states FOUR, who have served 16 years. In this, Gen. Harrison's whole term of four years is reckoned. What is also worthy of remark, is, that no Northern President has served more than one term.

Next in importance to the President is the office of Secretary of State, as he manages all the business and correspondence with foreign courts, instructs our foreign ministers, and negotiates all treaties. Of the 15 who have filled this office, up to 1845, the Slave states have had 10, who have served 37 years; the Free states 5, who have served 19 years.

Note No. X.

In nothing is the gross injustice practised towards the Free states, more conspicuous than in the persons employed in those civil executive offices, at the city of Washington, and in those Diplomatic and Consular stations abroad, where the compensation is by salary. In the following list we give the persons employed in a few of the States, with their salaries, and the number of free white inhabitants of the respective States.

	Persons.	Salaries. Dols.	Free population.
Virginia	114	200,395	740,968
New York	37	63,250	2,378,890
Maryland	133	170,305	318,204
Pennsylvania	90	123,790	1,676,115
District of Co.	99	77,455	30,657
Massachusetts	43	86,245	729,030
Kentucky	7	34,150	590,253
Ohio	6	4,400	1,502,122

Note No. XI.

The Judiciary is the balance-wheel of our government. It takes cognizance of questions of the highest earthly moment—questions of constitutional law—questions of chartered rights and privileges—questions involving millions of property—and, above all, questions that *decide the liberty and slavery of man*. If there be any spot, therefore, that should be free from sectional bias, it is the Supreme Court of the United States, the judges of which should be appointed, not only for their high legal attainments and integrity, but with reference to the number of inhabitants, and, consequently, to the legal interests of the different parts of the country. But how entirely opposite has been the practice. Of the 30 Judges of that Court, the Slave states have had 17; the Free states, 13; and that, too, while the free inhabitants of the Slave states are but about four and a half millions; the inhabitants of the Free states nine and a half millions—more than double.

Then look at the most unjust manner in which the circuits are divided. Vermont, Connecticut, and New York, with 42 representatives in Congress, and a free population of over *three millions*, constitute one circuit; while Alabama and Louisiana, with but 11 representatives, and a free population of but *half a million*, constitute another circuit. New Jersey and Pennsylvania, with a population of *two millions*, constitute the third circuit. Mississippi and Arkansas, with a free population of but *half a million*, constitute the ninth circuit. We say *free* population, because the poor slave has nothing to do with courts of law, having no *legal* rights to maintain.

Lastly, observe the same inequality and injustice, carried out in the salaries of the Judges. Louisiana, with a free population of 183,959, has one Judge at a salary of 3000 dollars; Ohio, with a population of 1,519,464, more than eight times as great as that of Louisiana, has only one Judge, at a salary of 1000: that is, while he has more than eight times as many people to do business for, he receives but one-third as much pay. Arkansas, with a free population of 77,639, has one Judge at a salary of 2000 dollars; New Hampshire, with a population of 284,573, has but one Judge, at a

salary of 1000 dollars. Mississippi, with a free population of 180,440, has one Judge, who receives 2500
dollars; Indiana, with a population of 685,863, has but
one Judge, who receives only 1000 dollars; receiving
but two-fifths as much pay for doing more than three
times the work.

Note No. XII.

The following is a portion of the Address of the
Pennsylvania Convention, held in Philadelphia, Feb.
22, 1844 :—

"The great object of the Liberty party is, in the
words of the Constitution, 'TO ESTABLISH JUSTICE; TO
SECURE THE BLESSINGS OF LIBERTY.' It is, ABSOLUTE
AND UNQUALIFIED DIVORCE OF THE GENERAL GOVERN-
MENT FROM ALL CONNECTION WITH SLAVERY. We would
say, in the fervent language of that noble son of freedom, CASSIUS M. CLAY, of Kentucky, 'Let the whole
North, in a mass, in conjunction with the patriotic of
the South, withdraw the moral sanction and legal power
of the Union from the sustainment of slavery.' We
would employ every CONSTITUTIONAL means to eradicate it from our entire country, because it would be
for the highest welfare of our entire country. We
would have liberty established in the District, and in all
the Territories. We would put a stop to the internal slave trade, pronounced, even by Thomas Jefferson Randolph, of Virginia, to be 'worse and more
odious than the foreign slave trade itself.' We would,
in the words of the Constitution, have 'the citizens
of each State have all the privileges and immunities of citizens in the several States;' and not, for

the color of their skin, be subjected to every indignity and abuse, and wrong, and even imprisonment.* We would have equal taxation. We would have the seas free. We would have a free and secure post-office. We would have liberty of speech and of the press, which the Constitution guarantees to us. We would have our members in Congress utter their thoughts freely, without threats from the pistol or the bowie-knife. We would have the right of petition most sacredly regarded. We would secure to every man what the Constitution secures, 'the right of trial by jury.' We would do what we can for the encouragement and improvement of the colored race. We would look to the best interests of the country, and the *whole* country, and not legislate for the good of an Oligarchy, the most arrogant that ever lorded it over an insulted people. We would have our commercial treaties with foreign nations regard the interests of the Free states. We would provide safe, adequate, and permanent markets for the produce of free labor. And, when reproached with slavery, we would be able to say to the world, with an open front and a clear conscience, our General Government has nothing to do with it, either to promote, to sustain, to defend, to sanction, or to approve."

Note No. XIII.

The following is a brief history of the several resolutions which have passed the House of Representa-

* Read the memorial of citizens of Boston, to the House of Representatives, on the imprisonment of free citizens of Massachusetts by the authorities of Savannah, Charleston, and New Orleans.

tives since 1836, against the consideration of any petitions respecting slavery. They are familiarly called " Gag Resolutions," and go by the name of the persons who introduced them.

Pinckney's Gag was passed May 26, 1836, by a majority of 46. Of the 117 yeas, 82 were from the Free states.

Hawes's Gag, January 18, 1837, by a majority of 58. Of the yeas, 70 were from the Free states.

Patton's Gag, December 31, 1838, by a majority of 48. Of the yeas, 52 were from the Free states.

Atherton's Gag, January 12, 1839, by a majority of 48. Of the yeas, 49 were from the Free states, AND ALL OF THE DEMOCRATIC PARTY.

Johnson's Gag, Jan. 28, 1840, by a majority of 6. Of the yeas, 28 were from the Free states, AND ALL BUT ONE OF THE DEMOCRATIC PARTY. But none of these " gags " would have been carried had it not been for SOUTHERN WHIGS. Of the yeas for Johnson's Gag, 40 were WHIGS FROM THE SLAVE STATES. This, as well as every other important subject of legislation in Congress for the last thirty years, shows clearly, that with the South, all party distinctions give way at once, at the bidding of slavery. When Northern men shall be as united for liberty as Southern men have been for slavery, how soon will our country be free from its present reproach !

NOTE No. XIV.

The Liberty party, at the Presidential election in 1840, gave 6983 votes; at the election in 1844, it gave 62,324 votes. Its growth has been regular, and as rapid as could be expected. It resorts to no unworthy means to increase its numbers, and desires others to join its ranks, only as they are convinced of the truth and righteousness of its principles.

Let it not, however, be despised for its yet comparatively small numbers. The great philosophical historian, Milman, says, "It is erroneous to estimate strength and influence by numerical calculation. All political changes are wrought by a compact, organized, and disciplined minority." This is the secret of the success of the slaveholders. They have controlled the government for the past fifty years, because they have been a "*compact, organized, and disciplined* minority." It is computed, on a careful estimate, that there are not more than 250,000 slaveholders in the land, and that of these, deducting widows, minors, and others, there are not more than 150,000 voters. When the Liberty party shall be "a compact, organized, and disciplined minority," of such a size, and shall control the counsels of the nation in favor of liberty, as the slaveholders now control them in favor of slavery, how soon will slavery die! Reader! will you not resolve that you will be one to help in bringing about such a glorious result?

Note No. XV.

To the question "what has the North to do with slavery?" no answer more satisfactory, and none more eloquent, certainly, can be given, than the following extract from a letter from Cassius M. Clay, dated Lexington, Kentucky, October 25th, 1845, to Messrs. C. D. Cleveland, J. Bouvier, W. Elder, and T. S. Cavender, a committee that forwarded to him a series of resolutions adopted at a meeting held in the State

House, in Philadelphia, to sympathize with him in the brutal assault made upon his press, and the violence threatened to his person, by the mob of the 18th of August :—

"The question has been again and again asked, in the most complacent simplicity, 'What has the free North to do with Slavery?' The Slave states added to the Union; the unconstitutional establishment of slavery in the district of Columbia; its unlawful sufferance in the territories, the high seas, and places of national, exclusive jurisdiction, answer, the North is as guilty of this crime against man's supremacy and immortality as the South; more so, because she is derelict in her duty, with far less temptation. But as no offence goes unpunished, she is reaping the fruit of her sorry policy, by the unjust and disgraceful wars in which she has been compelled to engage—by taxes which have been imposed upon her—by the immense capital which has been swallowed up in Southern bankruptcy—by the hanging of citizens without trial by jury and without law—by the imprisonment of her seamen—by the expulsion of, and insult to, her ambassadors—by the denial of justice in courts of national justice—and, lastly, by the impudent seizure and forcible abduction of her own freeborn citizens upon her own soil, and their incarceration in distant prisons. Shall any one be so base as any longer to ask, 'What has the North to do with Slavery?' or, rather, shall not the cry henceforth for ever, until the end, be, 'What shall the North do, to have nothing to do with Slavery?'"

Again, in the same letter, speaking of the threats uttered against himself, and the attack upon the freedom of the press, he says :--

"If this be an unnecessary infliction of the slave power, I call upon the nation to relieve me. If it be a necessary woe, following in the wake of American slavery, then, by all that is sacred among men, or holy in heaven, let AMERICANS RISE IN THE OMNIPOTENCY OF THE BALLOT, and say, SLAVERY SHALL DIE ! "

That is the true doctrine. Let all the citizens of the Free states, and all the non-slaveholders in the Slave states, RISE IN THE OMNIPOTENCY OF THE BALLOT, AND SAY, SLAVERY SHALL DIE.

NOTE No. XVI.

According to the Constitution, DIRECT TAXES must be apportioned among the several States in the ratio of their representation; and as the slave representatives would increase this number, it would also increase the amount of the tax in the same ratio. But mark how the slaveholders have escaped the consequence of this "compromise." The whole net revenue of our Government, from the 4th of March, 1789, to January 1, 1845, has amounted to about 975 millions of dollars; of which but little more than 12 millions have been received in direct taxes; and of this, the South has paid for her slave representation only 1,256,553 dollars, or about one million and a quarter. But had the revenue of the Government, amounting to

975 millions, been raised by direct taxation, the South would have had to pay, as her proportion, for her slave representation, over 105 millions; but instead of that she has paid but one million and a quarter.

When, therefore, at the close of the last war, our country was in debt about 120 millions of dollars, the South resolved that this should not be paid by direct taxes, but by duties laid upon imported goods. Accordingly the Tariff of 1816 was established. It was then emphatically a Southern measure. That Tariff, for instance, admitted the articles used for the clothing of slaves at a duty of *five cents* on the dollar's worth, and charged *twenty cents* on the dollar's worth of finer articles used for the clothing of free laborers, thereby making the honest labor of the Free states pay *four* dollars, while the slave labor of the Slave states paid but *one*, for clothing.

The Free states, however, with their industry and skill, soon accommodated themselves to this state of things, and their manufactures, by degrees, rose to a height of great prosperity. But no sooner was our national debt paid, than the South, ever watchful of its purpose, resolved to strike a death-blow at the prosperity of the Free states; and, accordingly, the celebrated "compromise" Tariff of 1832 was devised and carried; in which the "compromise" was, as it ever has been, *all one way*. Nothing is clearer than that the Slave power put on the Tariff in 1816, and took it off in 1832. They have done just as they pleased. Reader, it is in your power to say, they shall do so no longer.

Note No. XVII.

The aggregate amount of the appropriations for THE NAVY, for three years previous to 1846, was 17,357,556 dollars, a considerable portion of which was spent for the HOME SQUADRON, which consisted, in 1843, of one frigate, three sloops of war, four brigs, one schooner, and one steamship. But why all this array of naval force on our own coast at a time of profound peace? Let the late Judge Upshur, a Secretary of the Navy, and a Virginian, answer. In his first report to Congress, he speaks of "those incursions from which so much evil is to be apprehended." Again: "The effect of these incursions on the SOUTHERN portion of our country would be disastrous in the extreme." And again: "The Southern naval stations *more especially,* require a large force for their security. A large number of arms is kept in each of them, which, by a sudden irruption of a class of PEOPLE WHO ARE NOT CITIZENS, might be seized and used for very disastrous purposes." Here, men of the Free states, you have the whole of it. Here you see how we are taxed to provide a force to keep the slaves of the Southern states from insurrection. "What has the North to do with slavery?"

Again: look at the Post-Office Department. How enormous were the rates of postage for fifty years; and even now (1845) they are by no means so low as they should be. But why those high rates? In order that the Free states, where there is so much more correspondence, might make up the loss the department sustained in the Slave states. In 1844, the Free states were a *gain* to the department of more than half a million of dollars, while the Slave states were a *loss* to the department of more than half a million. The Liberty party will not cease in their efforts in this matter, till the postage here is the same as it is in England; TWO CENTS, PREPAID BY STAMPS, FOR ALL DISTANCES, ON EVERY LETTER WEIGHING HALF AN OUNCE. What comfort and joy would this bring to the door of every farmer, tradesman, mechanic, merchant, and professional man throughout the land !

Again: see how we were taxed to support the Florida war. That war, so disgraceful to our country, cost FORTY MILLIONS of dollars ; and it was undertaken, prosecuted, and finished, solely for the benefit of the slaveholder, that the slave, escaping from his tyranny, might not find protection in the wigwam of the red man. It was for this that the decree went forth, that the Indian must be driven from his native forests ; and the foul deed was done. " What has the North to do with slavery ?"

Note No. XVIII.

Of the 43 officers in the Navy Department in Washington, in 1844, there were 31 from the Slave states, and but 12 from the Free states : and of all the officers in the Navy, whether in actual service or waiting orders, Pennsylvania, with a free population more than double that of Virginia, had but 177, while Virginia had 224.

Note No. XIX.

Never was this policy of the slaveholders more conspicuous than in filling the vacancy on the bench of the Supreme Court, occasioned by the death of Judge Thompson, in December, 1843. Two or three most able and upright men were rejected by the Senate, because it was feared that they had sentiments adverse to slavery. And how tame, on all such occasions, have been the Senators from the Free states! But such instances might be multiplied indefinitely.

NOTE No. XX.

See the letter of instructions written by Daniel Webster, as Secretary of State, to Edward Everett, our minister at London, respecting the slaves shipwrecked in the brig Creole; a letter of such a character as to receive a deservedly severe review from an independent and able editor of the Secretary's own party—Charles King, of the New York American.

NOTE No. XXI.

In 1790, Virginia, with about 70,000 square miles of territory, contained a population of 748,308; New York, with about 45,000 square miles of territory, contained a population of 340,120, not one half. In 1840, Virginia had 1,239,797; New York, 2,428,921, nearly double. In 1800, Kentucky had 220,955 inhabitants; Ohio, 45,365 : in 1840, the former had increased to 779,828; the latter, to 1,519,467 inhabitants. In Virginia there are 12 free inhabitants to a square mile; in New York, 52.

NOTE No. XXII.

According to the last census there are of scholars in free schools, in the Free states, 432,173; in the Slave states, 35,580. Ohio alone has 51,812 such scholars, more than are to be found in all the 13 Slave states.

In 1837, Governor Campbell reported to the Virginia legislature, that from the return of 98 clerks, it appeared that of 4614 applications for marriage licenses, no less than 1047 were made by MEN UNABLE TO WRITE! How admirably calculated to assume the responsibilities of the father!

NOTE No. XXIII.

SHIPPING, value of, in the Free states	. . . .	dols.	6,311,805
„ „ Slave states			704,291
MANUFACTURES, value in the Free states	. . .		334,139,690
„ „ Slave states			83,935,742

NOTE No. XXIV.

" From long-continued and close observation, we believe that the moral and religious condition of the slaves is such, that they may justly be considered the HEATHEN of this Christian country, and will bear comparison with heathen in any country in the world. The negroes are destitute of the Gospel, and ever will be under the present state of things."—*Report published by the Synod of South Carolina and Georgia, December 3, 1833.*

The Rev. C. C. Jones, in a sermon preached before two associations of planters in Georgia, thus writes: " Generally speaking they (the slaves) appear to us to be without God and without hope in the world ; a NATION OF HEATHENS in our very midst."

In the 10th Annual Report of the Sunday School Union, we see that there were that year in the Free states 504,835 scholars; and in the Slave states 82,532. The single state of New York had 161,768 about twice as many as all the Slave states together.

NOTE No. XXV.

The following table shows the force that each of the thirteen States supplied for the regular army from 1775 to 1783 inclusive, and also, the sums allowed to the several States for expenses incurred during the Revolutionary War.

States.	Troops furnished.	Money allowed.
New Hampshire,	dols. 12,497	dols. 4,278,015
Massachusetts,	67,907	17,964,613
Rhode Island,	5,908	3,782,974
Connecticut,	31,939	9,285,737
New York,	17,781	7,179,982
New Jersey,	10,726	5,342,770
Pennsylvania,	25,678	14,137,076
Total of the present seven Free states,	172,436	61,971,167
Delaware,	2,386	839,319
Maryland,	13,912	7,568,145
Virginia,	26,678	19,085,981
North Carolina,	7,263	10,427,586
South Carolina,	6,417	11,523,299
Georgia,	2,679	2,993,800
Total of the present six Slave states.	59,335	52,438,130

Besides this, it might be added, that of the 45 officers

of the revolutionary army, the seven Northern States furnished 30, the six Southern States 15.

By this table it will be seen, that while the Northern States furnished about three times the number of troops furnished by the Southern States, they received not one-fifth more money. North Carolina, South Carolina, and Georgia, furnished but 16,359 troops, and received about 25 millions of dollars; New York furnished 17,781 troops, and received but 7 millions. Virginia received over a million of dollars more than Massachusetts, while she furnished but a little more than one-third the number of soldiers.

Note No. XXVI.

The following extract from a speech of the Mayor of New Orleans indicates what power is felt to lie in the ballot-box. " So long as the people at the North contented themselves with the *name* of Abolitionists, we of the South had nothing to fear, but now that they carry the subject to the ballot-box, we have reason to tremble for the safety of our institutions."

Note No. XXVII.

Another instance of gross injustice that occurs to us, is the Distribution of the Surplus Revenue, by the Act of 1836. The sum to be distributed was 37,468,859 dollars; and the act declared that it should be divided in proportion to the representation of the several States in Congress. Of this, the South, with a free population of 3,789,674, received 16,058,082 dollars; while the North, with a free population of 7,003,229, received but 21,410,777 dollars. So that for each inhabitant of the free North there was but 3.05 dollars, while for each *free* person of the South there was received 4.23 dollars; or 1.18 dollars more for each free person in the South, than for each free person in the North. Consequently, the South, by this operation alone, received for her slave representation in Congress more than FOUR MILLIONS OF DOLLARS.

But what makes the injustice of this distribution still more flagrant, is the fact, that the surplus revenue was mostly accumulated by Northern industry and enterprise; first, from the duties on imported merchandise, of which the North pays three dollars to one paid by the South; and second, from the sales of the public lands, which are mostly bought by settlers from the Free states. So that, in short, while the Free states were mainly instrumental in accumulating the surplus revenue, in its distribution the Slave states received more than their just share by over FOUR MILLIONS OF DOLLARS! Who will now ask, "What has the North to do with slavery?"

NOTE No. XXVIII.

The following is the concluding paragraph of the Address of the great Liberty Convention of the Friends of Freedom in the Eastern and Middle States, held in Boston, October 1, 2, and 3, 1845.

"And, now, men of the free North!—Citizens of the Eastern and Middle States!—by every consideration of religion, humanity and patriotism, you are urged to the exertion of *all* your powers for the overthrow of slavery. Your homes and your altars, your honor and good name, are at stake. The slave in his prison stretches his manacled hands towards you, imploring your aid. A cloud of witnesses surrounds you. The oppressed millions of Europe beseech you to remove from their pathway to freedom the reproach and stumbling-block of Democratic slavery. From the damp depths of dungeons —from the stake and the scaffold, where the martyrs of liberty have sealed their testimony with their blood— solemn and awful voices call upon you to make the dead letter of your republicanism a living truth. Join with us, then, fellow citizens. Slavery is mighty : but it can be overthrown. In the name of God and humanity, let us bring the mighty ballot-box of a kingless people to bear upon it. The model man of our Republic, who might have been a king, but would not, calls from his grave upon each of us to do that, which he solemnly declared himself ready to do—to give his vote to free the slave and to abolish the wicked phantasy of property in man. He shall not call in vain. We acknowledge the duty of consecrating our votes to the deliverance of the oppressed, and joyfully do we perform it."

ADDENDA.

LETTER TO THE MANAGERS OF THE PHILADELPHIA BIBLE SOCIETY.

PREFATORY NOTE.

To the foregoing Addresses I append the following "Letter to the Managers of the Philadelphia Bible Society," for the following chief reasons.

First, because the PHILADELPHIA Address has always, in my mind, been intimately associated with the LETTER, bearing to it, as it does, the relation of cause and effect.[*]

Second, because it contains a quotation from a letter of the author of the CINCINNATI Address, showing his noble sentiments upon the duty of giving the Bible to the slave, at a time when public opinion upon the subject was such, that even the American Bible Society would not receive a separate fund for the purpose of supplying our slave population with the Scriptures.

Third, because, as my letter was not put upon the minutes of the Society, probably on account of its length, it may at some future time be asked why I presented my resignation as their President, and why it was accepted. This letter and the action of the Society upon it give the answer.

Fourth, because, at that time, no other paper to which I applied would give my letter a place in its columns, but the "American Anti-Slavery Reporter;" and hence, though it was copied into the "British and Foreign Anti-Slavery Reporter," but few in our country ever saw it. I feel, therefore,

---

[*] The "Address" appeared in the latter part of April; the "Letter" was sent on the third of June.

that justice to myself demands that it be put in a form more permanent as well as more accessible.

Fifth, because the action of the Bible Society upon my resignation is a fair exponent of the position of the Christian Church at that time upon the subject of Slavery. The managers represented the most prominent denominations of Christians in our city, and not only had the full confidence of their respective churches, but stood high in the estimation of the community at large. When they, therefore, felt it to be their duty virtually to eject their President from his office on account of his anti-slavery views so publicly expressed, it is conclusive evidence what was the prevailing sentiment of Christians on the subject in 1844; and it seems to me that this their action should have a record in the page of history.

I would only add that, though I feel, of course, unspeakable joy that the spirit of liberty is *now* so triumphant in our land, and that the principles once so generally odious are now the settled convictions of the best and largest portion of the nation, I reprint this letter in no unkind or retaliatory spirit towards those to whom it is addressed. I felt, indeed, at the time, deeply grieved at the course taken by the managers of the Society, but I never either impugned their motives or harbored the least feelings of resentment towards them, believing that they verily thought they ought thus to act in order to advance the best good of the Society whose highest interests and usefulness it was their duty to promote and extend. But whether their action then was right or wrong, and whether or not the end justified the means, I am now more than willing to leave to the calm judgment of an enlightened Christian public, at this, or at any future time.

C. D. C.

May, 1867.

MANAGERS OF THE PHILADELPHIA
BIBLE SOCIETY.

Philadelphia,
3rd June, 1844.

CHRISTIAN BRETHREN,

IIEREWITH tender to you my resignation as President of the Philadelphia
Bible Society. To that post of honor
and responsibility, in one of the great departments of Christian benevolence, I was elected in
November, 1839. What the Society did for the years
previous, and what it has done since; what changes,
beneficial or otherwise, have been introduced; how
many or how few plans have been devised and executed,
for engaging the earnest co-operation of Christians of
all denominations throughout the sphere of our labors;
how much or how little agency I may have had in what
has been done; how much or how little I may have
labored in the many ways in which such a cause calls
for continuous and efficient action;—of all these things
I have, of course, nothing to say. The record of a part,

though but a part, is before you. It has become history, and history it will remain.

And here, wishing you, as a Society, all wisdom in the choice of my successor; still greater success in all your future plans of benevolence; and for each of you individually the richest of all blessings—here I might close. But that plainness and Christian candour which, I trust, will ever characterize me through life, and which, at such a time, are due alike to you and to myself, demand that I should say something more.

Ever since you elected me to be your President, it has been my fixed purpose that I would continue such no longer, certainly, than it appeared I held the office by the unanimous wish of the board. If there be any place where entire confidence, entire harmony, entire love should prevail, it is where Christians meet together to devise plans for the circulation of that Word, the very essence of which is love and good-will to man. Not that all the Board should have precisely the same views in morals, religion, or politics. To require that, or to expect that, would be as absurd as to require or to expect that all should look alike, or be of the same stature. While each claims for himself the right to hold his own opinions upon all subjects without being amenable to the Board, each should have the justice and magnanimity, as well as Christian charity, to allow the same to all other members, never dreaming that diversities of opinion in individuals conflict with their duties as managers, or commit the Board in the slightest degree to their own peculiar views. But it seems that the time has arrived when there is to be an exception to this clear rule of action.

On the 17th of last month, when calling on one of the

vice-presidents, to consult with him, as one of the committee, in relation to our anniversary, he said that he felt it to be his duty, as my friend, to say that a number of members of the Board had within a few days expressed opinions adverse to my being re-elected the President of the Society; and that there would doubtless be many votes given against me at the next election, or words to that effect. The ground of the opposition, he said, was the charge of my being the author of "The Address of the Liberty Party of Pennsylvania to the People of the State." To that charge, with however much of odium it may be attended in this community, I would here plead guilty. But how it was that my being the author of that "Address" conflicted with my duties as your President did not, I confess, so readily appear. The thought immediately occurred to me that the most prominent member of the Pennsylvania Bible Society is, and has been for many years, a slaveholder. I say it not in the least spirit of unkindness to that gentleman, but merely state it as a fact, with which I know many of you are familiar. Yet I never heard it whispered even, that such a relation constituted any objection to his being, year after year, elected to the responsible office of corresponding secretary.

How, then, my being the author of an Address to the people of Pennsylvania advocating the eternal principles of truth and justice—an Address, every moral sentiment of which is, I believe, in accordance with the truths of that Bible which we have been laboring to spread—an Address which calls upon all good men to exert their influence to elect such rulers as have the fear of God before their eyes—an Address which holds up one man,

L

the idol of a great party, in the light in which every moral man, not to say Christian, should view him—an Address which speaks of slavery as Christian men, in growing numbers, all over the world are speaking of it, whose moral vision is not obscured by the thousand selfish interests that ensnare the soul and lead captive the understanding—how, I say, my being the author of such an Address disqualified me from being the President of a Bible society did not, I confess, appear so plain to me.

It is enough for me, however, to have been assured that a considerable portion of the Board seem to think so; and therefore, agreeably to the resolution always formed in my own mind, to preside over you no longer than it seemed to be desired by a wish unanimous or approximating to unanimity, I deem it best to retire from your body, that you may select some one to fill my place in whom you can all harmoniously unite.

Allow me, however, to say that there are some questions connected with this subject, entirely independent of myself, which it may be well for the Board to ask and seriously to ponder. Are they prepared, as a body, before the world, to take what will seem to be pro-slavery ground, in deeming one unfit any longer to preside over them from his anti-slavery views? Are they prepared in this day of increasing Christian light, and in the face of the Christian public, to do anything that would seem, in the slightest degree, to countenance or strengthen a corrupt sentiment on the subject of slavery? What, then, I ask, will be thought of the offering up, as a peace-offering, a brother as a sacrifice upon the altar of its Moloch? I ask not what a Christian public, merely, may think of such things; but I ask what will high-

minded men think? Will it not seem to them something like persecution for opinion's sake? and will it
meet their sense of right action, to have anyone, though
they might not agree with him in sentiment, removed
from a responsible station, for writing what he has
written under a deep sense of duty and responsibility.

Such are a few questions which the Board may here
ask. Others of a similar character will doubtless present themselves.

Let it be here borne in mind, brethren, that I have
never asked you to espouse the opposite side; that I have
never asked you to take anti-slavery ground, except by
doing all you could to circulate the best of all anti-
slavery books—the BIBLE. You will bear me witness
that, notwithstanding my well-known views on the
subject of Slavery, I have never introduced them into
the Board. Not that I was prevented by any considerations of unpopularity. Were I governed by such
low motives, I never, in Philadelphia certainly, should
have written that Address—no, nor ever have divulged
the sentiments I hold. But having thought often and
deeply upon the course which it was duty for me to
take, I never could see what good could be done by
bringing the subject of Slavery before our Board, limited
as our sphere of operations is to the city and districts.
I have lamented, indeed, and deeply lamented, that the
American Bible Society, in its annual report, when
giving its estimate of the destitution of our country, has
never mentioned the poor down-trodden slave. I have
thought the course pursued by that society as yielding
to the prevailing corrupt sentiment of the day, certainly
not in keeping with the spirit of the Gospel.

And here I am glad to be able to present to you some
high confirmation of my views. My early and honored
friend, S. P. Chase, Esq., of Cincinnati, for many years
the efficient president of the Young Men's Bible Society
of that city, one of the most prominent members of the
Liberty party in Ohio, and who needs no eulogy of
mine to his moral and intellectual worth, in a letter
dated May 28th, 1843, thus writes :—

" Our Young Men's Bible Society and yours, are
" two most important auxiliaries. Can we not do
" something to arouse the American Bible Society
" from its apathy in regard to the destitution of
" the Slaves? When they propose to put a Bible
" in every family, and omit all reference to the
" Slaves; and when, giving an account of the
" destitution of the land, they make no mention
" of two and a half millions of people perishing
" in our midst, without the Scriptures, can
" we help feeling that something is dreadfully
" wrong?"

This, brethren, is a most solemn question. It is a
question which I verily believe the Board of the
American Bible Society, so far as they may have
yielded, directly or indirectly, openly or silently, to a
corrupt public sentiment on this subject, will have to
answer at the bar of Him who has declared, that " if
ye have respect to persons, ye commit sin;" and that
"inasmuch as ye did it not to one of the least of these,
ye did it not to me." The spirit of Christianity is a
spirit of universal love and philanthropy. She looks
down with pity, and, if she could, she would look with

scorn upon all the petty distinctions that exist among men. She casts her benignant eye abroad over the earth, and, wherever she sees man, she sees him *as man*, as a being made in the image of God, whether an Indian, an African, or a Caucasian sun may shine upon him. She stoops from heaven to raise the fallen, to bind up the broken-hearted, to release the oppressed, to give liberty to the captive, and to break the fetters of those that are bound. She is marching onward with accelerated step, and, wherever she leaves the *true* impress of her heavenly influence, the moral wilderness is changed into the garden of the Lord. May it never be ours to do what may seem to be even the slightest obstacle to her universal sway.

Such, brethren, are a few of the many interesting thoughts that crowd upon me on this occasion. But I have already written more than I intended, and I cannot enlarge. In bringing this communication to a close, allow me to express to you individually, and as a Board, my most sincere Christian attachment. Whatever course any members may have taken in relation to this matter, I must believe that they have acted from what has seemed to them a sense of duty. Far be it from me to impeach their motives. Time, the great test of truth, may show them their course in a very different light from that in which they now view it. I may, as a Christian, lament that their views of duty are not more in unison with my own. I may, as a man, feel heart-sickened at the diseased, the deplorably diseased state of the public mind, in relation to two and a half millions of my fellow-men in bondage. I may, as a citizen of a Free state, blush at the humiliating fact, that not only the tyranny, but the ubiquity of the slave power is everywhere so manifest; that it has insinuated itself into our free domain to such a degree, that there seems to be as much mental Slavery in the Free states, as there is personal in the Slave states. I may feel all this, but I must not impeach the motives by which others have been governed.

And now let me, in conclusion, leave those points in which some of us may differ, and look only to those in which we have all agreed. Let me recur to pleasing recollections. Let me look back to the past five years, during which time we have all moved on so harmoniously together in our labors to furnish the destitute with the volume of Divine truth. I can truly say that our action together has ever been to me one continued source of pleasure. If there have been differences of opinion (and these have been very few and very slight) they have been settled as Christians always should settle them, in the kindest and most confiding manner. I thank you for all your kindness to me. I thank you for your confidence so early shown and so long continued. I thank you for the cordial support you have ever given to the various measures proposed to increase the resources and to extend the usefulness of our Society. And let me assure you, that of all the pleasing reminiscences of my life none will ever be to me sources of more grateful meditation, than those connected with the five years in which we have moved on, hand in hand, so harmoniously together. If, during those years, in our labors to carry the Gospel to the destitute, we have been the humble instruments of bringing even one sinner to turn from the error of his ways; of giving even to one those consolations which the Bible alone can give, we may feel, indeed, most richly rewarded for any amount of time or of labor we may have devoted to the work.

Again, wishing you from my heart, individually, and as a Board, the richest of Heaven's blessings,

I remain, very sincerely,

Your friend and brother,

CHARLES DEXTER CLEVELAND.

As soon as the Secretary, Mr. John Sparhawk, had read the foregoing letter, he offered a resolution that my resignation be *not* accepted. A long debate thereon ensued, but the resolution was lost by the decisive vote of seven to fourteen. A counter resolution was then offered that my resignation be accepted " with regret," which was carried, fourteen to seven. Theodore Cuyler, Esq. then offered the following, which was carried unanimously, the whole number of managers present —twenty-one—voting *aye.*

" Resolved,—That this Board are mainly indebted to " Professor C. D. Cleveland for the prominent and in- " fluential position it has attained in the regards of this " Christian community, and that they bear an earnest " testimony to the sound judgment and unwearied zeal " which have ever characterized the discharge of his " duties in his responsible office."

THE END.

CHISWICK PRESS :—PRINTED BY WHITTINGHAM AND WILKINS,
TOOKS COURT, CHANCERY LANE.

A List of Books

SAMPSON LOW, SON, AND MARSTON.

MILTON HOUSE, LUDGATE HILL, LONDON.

❧

** When the price is not given, the work was not ready at the time of issuing this list.

[*October*, 1866.

NEW ILLUSTRATED WORKS.

TWO CENTURIES OF SONG ; or, Melodies Madrigals, Sonnets, and other Occasional Verse of the English Poets of the last 200 years. With Critical and Biographical Notes by Walter Thornbury. Illustrated by Original Pictures of Eminent Artists, Drawn and Engraved especially for this work. Printed on toned paper, with coloured borders, designed by Henry Shaw, F.S.A. Very handsomely bound with clasp, price One Guinea ; morocco, 2*l*. 2*s*.

BISHOP HEBER'S HYMNS. An Illustrated Edition, with upwards of one hundred Designs. Engraved, in the first style of Art under the superintendence of J. D. Cooper. Small 4to. handsomely, bound, price Half a Guinea ; morocco, 18*s*.

MILTON'S PARADISE LOST. With the original Steel Engravings of John Martin. Printed on large paper, royal 4to. handsomely bound, 3*l*. 13*s*. 6*d*.

POEMS OF THE INNER LIFE. Selected chiefly from modern Authors, by permission. Small 8vo. 6*s*. ; gilt, 6*s*. 6*d*.

THE DIVINE AND MORAL SONGS OF DR. WATTS : a New and very choice Edition. Illustrated with One Hundred Woodcuts in the first style of the Art, from Original Designs by Eminent Artists, engraved by J. D. Cooper. Small 4to. cloth extra, price 7*s*. 6*d*. ; morocco, 15*s*.

CHOICE EDITIONS OF CHOICE BOOKS. New Editions. Illustrated by C. W. Cope, R.A., T. Creswick, R.A., Edward Duncan, Birket Foster, J. C. Horsley, A.R.A., George Hicks, R. Redgrave, R.A., C. Stonehouse, F. Tayler, George Thomas, H. J. Townshend, E. H. Wehnert, Harrison Weir, &c. Crown 8vo. cloth, 5*s*. each ; mor. 10*s*. 6*d*.

Bloomfield's Farmer's Boy.	Keat's Eve of St. Agnes.
Campbell's Pleasures of Hope.	Milton's l'Allegro.
Cundall's Elizabethan Poetry.	Roger's Pleasures of Memory.
Coleridge's Ancient Mariner.	Shakespeare's Songs and Sonnets.
Goldsmith's Deserted Village.	Tennyson's May Queen.
Goldsmith's Vicar of Wakefield.	Wordsworth's Pastoral Poems.
Gray's Elegy in a Churchyard.	

THE GREAT SCHOOLS OF ENGLAND. A History of the Foundation, Endowments, and Discipline of the chief Seminaries of Learning in England ; including Eton, Winchester, Westminster, St. Paul's, Charterhouse, Merchant Taylors', Harrow, Rugby, Shrewsbury, &c ; with notices of distinguished Scholars. By Howard Staunton, Esq. With numerous Illustrations. One volume 8vo., handsomely bound in cloth, price 12*s*.

Life in the Pyrenees. By Henry Blackburn, Esq., Author of "Travelling in Spain in the Present Day." With upwards of 100 Illustrations by Gustave Doré. 8vo.

Pictures of English Life; illustrated by Ten folio page Illustrations on wood, by J. D. Cooper, after Drawings by R. Barnes and E. M. Whimperis, with appropriate descriptive Poems, printed in floreated borders. Imperial folio, cloth extra, 14s.

Favourite English Poems. *Complete Edition.* Comprising a Collection of the most celebrated Poems in the English Language, with but one or two exceptions unabridged, from Chaucer to Tennyson. With 300 Illustrations by the first Artists. Two vols. royal 8vo. half bound, top gilt, Roxburgh style, 1l. 18s.; antique calf, 3l. 3s.

. Either Volume sold separately as distinct works. 1. " Early English Poems, Chaucer to Dyer." 2. " Favourite English Poems, Thomson to Tennyson." Each handsomely bound in cloth, 1l. 1s.

" *One of the choicest gift-books of the year,* " *Favourite English Poems*" *is not a toy book, to be laid for a week on the Christmas table and then thrown aside with the sparkling trifles of the Christmas tree, but an honest book, to be admired in the season of pleasant remembrances for its artistic beauty; and, when the holydays are over, to be placed for frequent and affectionate consultation on a favourite shelf.*"—Athenæum.

Schiller's Lay of the Bell. Sir E. Bulwer Lytton's translation; beautifully illustrated by forty-two wood Engravings, drawn by Thomas Scott, and engraved by J. D. Cooper, after the Etchings by Retszch. Oblong 4to. cloth extra, 14s.; morocco, 25s.

The Poetry of Nature. Selected and Illustrated with Thirty-six Engravings by Harrison Weir. Small 4to. handsomely bound in cloth, gilt edges, 12s.; morocco, 1l. 1s.

Pictures of Society, Grave and Gay; comprising One Hundred Engravings on Wood. Handsomely bound in cloth, with an elaborate and novel Design, by Messrs. Leighton and Co. Royal 8vo. price 21s.

An Entirely New Edition of Edgar A. Poe's Poems. Illustrated by Eminent Artists. Small 4to. cloth extra, price 10s. 6d.

A History of Lace, from the Earliest Period; with upwards of One Hundred Illustrations and Coloured Designs. By Mrs. Bury Palliser. One volume, 8vo. choicely bound in cloth. 31s. 6d.

LITERATURE WORKS OF REFERENCE, AND EDUCATION.

THE English Catalogue of Books: giving the date of publication of every book published from 1835 to 1863, in addition to the title, size, price, and publisher, in one alphabet. An entirely new work, combining the Copyrights of the " London Catalogue" and the " British Catalogue." One thick volume of 900 pages, half morocco, 45s.

Elegant Sonnets; being Selections, with an Essay on Sonnets and Sonneteers, by the late Leigh Hunt. Edited, from the original MS., with additions, by S. Adams Lee. 2 vols.

A Concordance to Milton's Poetical Works. By Charles D. Cleveland, Author of " The Compendium of English, American, and Classical Literature." Crown 8vo.

Celebrated Letters, based on W. Holcombe's Literature in Letters. Selected and arranged, with Critical and Biographical Notes, by William Moy Thomas. Crown 8vo.

The Gentle Life: Essays in Aid of the Formation of Character of Gentlemen and Gentlewomen. Crown 8vo. Seventh Edition, 6s.; calf antique, 12s.

A Second Volume of the Gentle Life. Uniform with the First Series. Second Edition, 6s.; calf antique, 12s.

About in the World: Essays uniform with, and by the author of "The Gentle Life." 3rd edition. Crown 8vo. 6s.; calf antique, 12s.

Essays by Montaigne. With Vignette Portrait. Small post 8vo. 6s.; calf antique, 12s.

Varia: Rare Readings from Scarce Books. Reprinted by permission from the *Saturday Review* and *Spectator*. Beautifully printed by Whittingham. Crown 8vo. cloth, 6s.; calf antique, 12s.

Spanish Papers, and other Miscellanies, hitherto unpublished or uncollected. By Washington Irving. Arranged and edited by Pierre M. Irving. 2 vols. 8vo. cloth, 24s.

Familiar Words; an Index Verborum, or Dictionary of Quotation of Sentences and Phrases which have become embedded in our English tongue. Second Edition, revised and enlarged. Crown 8vo. 6s.; calf antique, 12s.

Like unto Christ. A new translation of the De Imitatione Christi, usually ascribed to Thomas à Kempis—forming a volume of *The Gentle Life* Series. Crown 8vo. 6s.; calf antique, 12s.

The Countess of Pembroke's Arcadia. By Sir Philip Sidney. Edited, with Notes, by the Author of "The Gentle Life." Crown 8vo.

The Silent Hour: Essays for Sunday Reading, Original and Selected. By the Author of "The Gentle Life." Crown 8vo.

Life Portraits of Shakspeare; with an Examination of the Authenticity, and a History of the various Representations of the Poet. Illustrated by Photographs of authentic and received Portraits. Square 8vo. 21s.; or with Photograph of the Will, 25s.

Richmond and its Inhabitants, from the Olden Time. With Memoirs and Notes by Richard Crisp. With Illustrations. Post 8vo. 10s. 6d.

The Complete Poetical Works of John Milton, with a Life of the Author: and a Verbal Index containing upwards of 20,000 references to all the Poems. By Charles Dexter Cleveland. New Edition. 8vo. 12s.

Her Majesty's Mails: a History of the Post Office, and an Industrial Account of its Present Condition. By Wm. Lewins, of the General Post Office. 2nd edition, revised, and enlarged, with a Photographic Portrait of Sir Rowland Hill. Small post 8vo. 6s.

A History of Banks for Savings; including a full account of the origin and progress of Mr. Gladstone's recent prudential measures. By William Lewins, Author of 'Her Majesty's Mails.' 8vo. cloth. 12s.

The Origin and History of the English Language, and of the early literature it embodies. By the Hon. George P. Marsh, U. S. Minister at Turin, Author of "Lectures on the English Language." 8vo. cloth extra, 16s.

Lectures on the English Language; forming the Introductory Series to the foregoing Work. By the same Author. 8vo. Cloth, 16s. This is the only author's edition.

Man and Nature; or, Physical Geography as Modified by Human Action. By George P. Marsh, Author of " Lectures on the English Language," &c. 8vo. cloth, 14s.

English and Scotch Ballads, &c. An extensive Collection. Designed as a Complement to the Works of the British Poets, and embracing nearly all the Ancient and Traditionary Ballads both of England and Scotland, in all the important varieties of form in which they are extant, with Notices of the kindred Ballads of other Nations. Edited by F. J. Child, new Edition, revised by the Editor. 8 vols. fcap. cloth, 3s. 6d. each.

The Handy-book of Patent and Copyright Law, English and Foreign. By James Fraser, Esq. Post 8vo. cloth, 4s. 6d.

A Concise Summary of the Law of English and French Copyright Law and International Law, by Peter Burke. 12mo. 5s.

Index to the Subjects of Books published in the United Kingdom during the last Twenty Years—1837-1857. Containing as many as 74,000 references, under subjects, so as to ensure immediate reference to the books on the subject required, each giving title, price, publisher, and date. Two valuable Appendices are also given—A, containing full lists of all Libraries, Collections, Series, and Miscellanies—and B, a List of Literary Societies, Printing Societies, and their Issues. One vol. royal 8vo. Morocco, 1l. 6s.

The American Catalogue, or English Guide to American Lite-rature; giving the full title of original Works published in the United States of America since the year 1800, with especial reference to the works of interest to Great Britain, with the size, price, place, date of publication, and London prices. With comprehensive Index. 8vo. 2s. 6d. Also Supplement, 1837-60. 8vo. 6d.

Dr. Worcester's New and Greatly Enlarged Dictionary of the English Language. Adapted for Library or College Reference, comprising 40,000 Words more than Johnson's Dictionary, and 250 pages more than the Quarto Edition of Webster's Dictionary. In one Volume, royal 4to. cloth, 1,834 pp. price 31s. 6d. Half russia, 2l. 2s. The Cheapest Book ever published.

" The volumes before us show a vast amount of diligence; but with Webster it is diligence in combination with fancifulness,—with Worcester in combination with good sense and judgment. Worcester's is the soberer and safer book, and may be pronounced the best existing English Lexicon."—*Athenæum.*

The Publishers' Circular, and General Record of British and Foreign Literature; giving a transcript of the title-page of every work published in Great Britain, and every work of interest published abroad, with lists of all the publishing houses.
Published regularly on the 1st and 15th of every Month, and forwarded post free to all parts of the world on payment of 8s. per annum.

The Ladies' Reader : with some Plain and Simple Rules and In-structions for a good style of Reading aloud, and a variety of Selections for Exercise. By George Vandenhoff, M.A., Author of " The Art of Elocution." Fcap. 8vo. Cloth, 5s.

The Clerical Assistant : an Elocutionary Guide to the Reading of the Scriptures and the Liturgy, several passages being marked for Pitch and Emphasis : with some Observations on Clerical Bronchitus. By George Vandenhoff, M.A. Fcap. 8vo. Cloth, 3s. 6d.

The Art of Elocution as an essential part of Rhetoric, with in-structions in Gesture, and an Appendix of Oratorical, Poetical and Dramatic extracts. By George Vandenhoff, M A. Third Edition. 5s.

Latin-English Lexicon, by Dr. Andrews. New Edition. 8vo. 18s.

The superiority of this justly-famed Lexicon is retained over all others by the fulness of its quotations, the including in the vocabulary proper names, the distinguishing whether the derivative is classical or otherwise, the exactness of the references to the original authors, and in the price.

" *Every page bears the impress of industry and care.*"—Athenæum.

" *The best Latin Dictionary, whether for the scholar or advanced student.*"—Spectator.

" *We never saw such a book published at such a price.*"—Examiner.

An English Grammar. By Matthew Green. New edition revised. 12mo. cloth, 1s. 6d.

The Farm and Fruit of Old. From Virgil. By a Market Gardener. 1s.

Usque ad Cœlum ; or, the Dwellings of the People. By Thomas Hare, Esq., Barrister-at-Law. Fcap. 1s.

A Few Hints on proving Wills, &c, without professional assistance. By a Probate-Court Official. Fcap. cloth, 6d.

Domestic Servants, their Duties and Rights. By a Barrister. 1s.

Signals of Distress, in Refuges and Houses of Charity ; in Industrial Schools and Reformatories ; at Invalids' Dinner Tables, and in the Homes of the Little Sisters of the Poor, &c. &c.; among the Fallen, the Vicious, and the Criminal ; where Missionaries travel, and where Good Samaritans clothe the naked. By Blanchard Jerrold, Author of " The Life of Douglas Jerrold," &c. Crown 8vo. 7s. 6d.

The Children of Lutetia ; or, Life amongst the Poor of Paris. By Blanchard Jerrold. 2 vols. post 8vo. cloth, 16s.

The Charities of London : an Account of the Origin, Operations, and general Condition of the Charitable, Educational, and Religious Institutions of London. 8th publication (commenced 1836). With Index. Fcap. [*Nearly ready.*

Prince Albert's Golden Precepts. *Second Edition*, with Photograph. A Memorial of the Prince Consort ; comprising Maxims and Extracts from Addresses of His late Royal Highness. Many now for the first time collected and carefully arranged. With an Index. Royal 16mo. beautifully printed on toned paper, cloth, gilt edges, 2s. 6d.

Our Little Ones in Heaven : Thoughts in Prose and Verse, selected from the Writings of favourite Authors ; with Frontispiece after Sir Joshua Reynolds. Fcap. 8vo. cloth extra, 3s. 6d.

NEW BOOKS FOR YOUNG PEOPLE.

THE TRUE HISTORY OF DAME PERKINS AND HER GREY MARE. Told for the Countryside and the Fireside. By Lindon Meadows. With Eight Coloured Illustrations by Phiz. Small 4to. cloth, 5s.

The Fire Ships. A Story by W. H. G. Kingston. Re-edited for Young People. With Illustrations. 5s.

The Frog's Parish Clerk ; and his Adventures in strange Lands. A Tale for young folk. By Thomas Archer. Numerous Illustrations. Small post 8vo. 5s.

Great Fun. Stories Told by Thomas Hood and Thomas Archer to 48 coloured pictures of Edward Wehnert. Beautifully printed in colours, 10s. 6d. Plain, 6s. well bound in cloth, gilt edges.

Or in Eight separate books, 1s. each, coloured. 6d. plain.

The Cherry-coloured Cat and her Three Friends.
The Live Rocking-Horse.
Master Mischief and Miss Meddle.
Cousin Nellie's Stories after School.
Harry High-Stepper.
Grandmamma's Spectacles.
How the House was Built.
Dog Toby and Artistical Arthur.

Under the Waves; or the Hermit Crab in Society. By Annie E. Ridley. Impl. 16mo. cloth extra, with coloured illustration. Cloth, 4s.; gilt edges, 4s. 6d.

Also beautifully Illustrated:—

Little Bird Red and Little Bird Blue. Coloured, 5s.
Snow-Flakes, and what they told the Children. Coloured, 5s.
Child's Book of the Sagacity of Animals. 5s.; coloured, 7s. 6d.
Child's Picture Fable Book. 5s.; or coloured, 7s. 6d.
Child's Treasury of Story Books. 5s.; or coloured, 7s. 6d.
The Nursery Playmate. 200 Pictures. 5s.; coloured, 9s.

The Boy's Own Book of Boats. By W. H. G. Kingston. Illustrations by E. Weedon, engraved by W. J. Linton. Fcap. 8vo. cloth, 5s. " *This well-written, well-wrought book.*"—Athenæum.

How to Make Miniature Pumps and a Fire-Engine: a Book for Boys. With Seven Illustrations. Fcap. 8vo. 1s.

The Cruise of the Frolic. By W. H. G. Kingston. Illustrated. Large fcap. 8vo. cloth, 5s.

Also by the same Author, well illustrated,

The Boy's Own Book of Boats. Illustrated by Weedon. 5s.
Ernest Bracebridge ; or, the Boy's Book of Sports. 5s.
Jack Buntline : the Life of a Sailor Boy. 2s.
The Fire Ships. 5s.

Vermont Vale; or, Home Pictures in Australia. By Maud Jeanne Franc. Small post 8vo, with a frontispiece, cloth extra, 5s.

Golden Hair; a Story for Young People. By Sir Lascelles Wraxall, Bart. With Eight full page Illustrations, 5s.

Also, same price, full of Illustrations :—

Black Panther : a Boy's Adventures among the Red Skins.
Life among the Indians. By George Catlin.
The Voyage of the Constance. By Mary Gillies.
Stanton Grange. By the Rev. C. J. Atkinson.
Boyhood of Martin Luther. By Henry Mayhew.
Stories of the Woods. From Cooper's Tales.
The Story of Peter Parley's own Life.

Noodle-doo. By the Author of "The Stories that Little Breeches told." With 16 large Engravings on Steel. Plain, 5s.; coloured, 7s. 6d.

Also, now ready, same size and price, and full of Illustrations.

Great Fun for our Little Friends. By Harriet Myrtle.
More Fun for our Little Friends. By the same Author.
The Book of Blockheads. By Charles Bennett.
The Stories that Little Breeches told. By the same Author.
Mr. Wind and Madame Rain. Illustrated by Charles Bennett.

Paul Duncan's Little by Little; a Tale for Boys. Edited by Frank Freeman. With an Illustration by Charles Keene. Fcap. 8vo. cloth 2s.; gilt edges, 2s. 6d. Also, same price,

Boy Missionary; a Tale for Young People. By Mrs. J. M. Parker.
Difficulties Overcome. By Miss Brightwell.
The Babes in the Basket: a Tale in the West Indian Insurrection.
Jack Buntline; the Life of a Sailor Boy. By W. H. G. Kingston.

The Swiss Family Robinson; or, the Adventures of a Father and Mother and Four Sons on a Desert Island. With Explanatory Notes and Illustrations. First and Second Series. New Edition, complete in one volume, 3s. 6d.

Geography for my Children. By Mrs. Harriet Beecher Stowe. Author of "Uncle Tom's Cabin," &c. Arranged and Edited by an English Lady, under the Direction of the Authoress. With upwards of Fifty Illustrations. Cloth extra, 4s. 6d.

Stories of the Woods; or, the Adventures of Leather-Stocking: A Book for Boys, compiled from Cooper's Series of "Leather-Stocking Tales." Fcap. cloth, Illustrated, 5s.
"I have to own that I think the heroes of another writer, viz. 'Leather-Stocking,' 'Uncas,' 'Hard Heart,' 'Tom Coffin,' are quite the equals of Sir Walter Scott's men;—perhaps 'Leather-Stocking' is better than any one in Scott's lot."—W. M. THACKERAY.

Child's Play. Illustrated with Sixteen Coloured Drawings by E. V. B., printed in fac-simile by W. Dickes' process, and ornamented with Initial Letters. New edition, with India paper tints, royal 8vo. cloth extra, bevelled cloth, 7s. 6d. The Original Edition of this work was published at One Guinea.

Child's Delight. Forty-two Songs for the Little Ones, with forty-two Pictures. 1s.; coloured, 2s. 6d.

Goody Platts, and her Two Cats. By Thomas Miller. Fcap. 8vo. cloth, 1s.

Little Blue Hood: a Story for Little People. By Thomas Miller, with coloured frontispiece. Fcap. 8vo. cloth, 2s. 6d.

Mark Willson's First Reader. By the Author of "The Picture Alphabet" and "The Picture Primer." With 120 Pictures. 1s.

The Picture Alphabet; or Child's First Letter Book. With new and original Designs. 6d.

The Picture Primer. 6d.

HISTORY AND BIOGRAPHY.

THE Conspiracy of Count Fieschi : an Episode in Italian History. By M. De Celesia. Translated by David Hilton, Esq., Author of a " History of Brigandage." With Portrait. 8vo.

A History of America, from the Declaration of Independence of the thirteen United States, to the close of the campaign of 1778. By George Bancroft ; forming the third volume of the History of the American Revolution. 8vo. cloth, 12s.   [*Just ready.*

A History of Brigandage in Italy; with Adventures of the more celebrated Brigands. By David Hilton, Esq. 2 vols. post 8vo. cloth, 16s.

A History of the Gipsies, with Specimens of the Gipsy Language. By Walter Simson. Post 8vo, 10s. 6d.

A History of West Point, the United States Military Academy and its Military Importance. By Capt. E. C. Boynton, A.M. With Plans and Illustrations. 8vo. 21s.

The Twelve Great Battles of England, from Hastings to Waterloo. With Plans, fcap. 8vo. cloth extra, 3s. 6d.

George Washington's Life, by Washington Irving. 5 vols. royal 8vo. 12s. each. Library Illustrated Edition. 5 vols. Imp. 8vo. 4l. 4s.

Plutarch's Lives. An entirely new Library Edition, carefully revised and corrected, with some Original Translations by the Editor. Edited by A. H. Clough, Esq. sometime Fellow of Oriel College, Oxford, and late Professor of English Language and Literature at University College. 5 vols. 8vo. cloth. 2l. 10s.
    " *Mr. Clough's work is worthy of all praise, and we hope that it will tend to revive the study of Plutarch.*"—Times.

Life of John Adams, 2nd President of the United States, by C. F. Adams. 8vo. 14s. Life and Works complete, 10 vols. 14s. each.

Life and Administration of Abraham Lincoln. Fcap. 8vo. stiff cover, 1s.; with map, speeches, &c. crown 8vo. 3s. 6d.

The Prison Life of Jefferson Davis ; embracing Details and Incidents in his Captivity, together with Conversations on Topics of great Public Interest. By John J. Craven, M.D.. Physician of the Prisoner during his Confinement. 1 vol. post 8vo. price 8s.

The Life and Correspondence of Benjamin Silliman, M.D., LL.D., late Professor of Chemistry, Mineralogy, and Geology in Yale College, U.S.A. Chiefly from his own MSS. and Diary. By George Fisher. With Portrait. 2 vols. post 8vo. price 24s.

Six Months at the White House with Abraham Lincoln : the Story of a Picture. By F. B. Carpenter. 12mo. 7s. 6d.

TRAVEL AND ADVENTURE.

WALK from London to the Land's End. By Elihu Burritt, Author of " A Walk from London to John O'Groats :" with several Illustrations. Large post 8vo. Uniform with the first edition of " John O'Groats." 12s.

A Walk from London to John O'Groats. With Notes by the Way. By Elihu Burritt. Second and cheaper edition. With Photographic Portrait of the Author. Small post 8vo. 6s.

Social Life of the Chinese : with some account of their religious, governmental, educational, and Business customs and opinions. By the Rev. Justus Doolittle. With over 100 Illustrations, in two vols. Demy 8vo. cloth, 24s.

Travelling in Spain in the Present Day. By Henry Blackburn. With numerous illustrations. Square post 8vo, cloth extra, 16s.

A Thousand Miles in the Rob Roy Canoe, or Rivers and Lakes of Europe. By John Macgregor, M.A. Fourth edition. With a map, and numerous Illustrations. Fcap. 8vo. cloth, 5s.

A Second Canoe Voyage in Norway, Sweden, &c. By John Macgregor, M.A. With a Map and numerous Illustrations. Fcap. 8vo.

Description of the New Rob Roy Canoe, built for a Voyage through Norway, Sweden, and the Baltic. Dedicated to the Canoe Club by the Captain. With Illustrations. Price 1s.

Captain Hall's Life with the Esquimaux. New and cheaper Edition, with Coloured Engravings and upwards of 100 Woodcuts. With a Map. Price 7s. 6d. cloth extra. Forming the cheapest and most popular Edition of a work on Arctic Life and Exploration ever published.
" *This is a very remarkable book, and unless we very much misunderstand both him and his book, the author is one of those men of whom great nations do well to be proud.*"—Spectator.

A Winter in Algeria, 1863-4. By Mrs. George Albert Rogers. With illustrations. 8vo. cloth, 12s.

Turkey. By J. Lewis Farley, F.S.S., Author of "Two Years in Syria." With Illustrations in Chromo-lithography, and a Portrait of His Highness Fuad Pasha. 8vo. 12s.

Letters on England. By Louis Blanc. 2 vols. post 8vo. 16s.

The Story of the Great March : a Diary of General Sherman's Campaign through Georgia and the Carolinas. By Brevet-Major G. W. Nichols, Aide-de-Camp to General Sherman. With a coloured Map and numerous Illustrations. 12mo. cloth, price 7s. 6d.

Arabian Days and Nights; or, Rays from the East: a Narrative. By Marguerite A. Power. 1 vol. Post 8vo. 10s. 6d.

Wild Scenes in South America; or, Life in the Llanos of Venezuela. By Don Ramon Paez. Numerous Illustrations. Post 8vo. cl. 10s. 6d.

The Prairie and Overland Traveller ; a Companion for Emigrants, Traders, Travellers, Hunters, and Soldiers, traversing great Plains and Prairies. By Capt. R. B. Marcey. Illustrated. Fcap. 8vo. cloth, 4s. 6d.

Home and Abroad (*Second Series*). A Sketch-book of Life, Men, and Travel, by Bayard Taylor. With Illustrations, post 8vo. cloth, 8s. 6d.

Northern Travel. Summer and Winter Pictures of Sweden, Lapland, and Norway, by Bayard Taylor. 1 vol. post 8vo., cloth, 8s. 6d.
Also by the same Author, each complete in 1 vol., with Illustrations.
Central Africa ; Egypt and the White Nile. 7s. 6d.
India, China, and Japan. 7s. 6d.
Palestine, Asia Minor, Sicily, and Spain. 7s. 6d.
Travels in Greece and Russia. With an Excursion to Crete. 7s. 6d.

After the War : a Southern Tour extending from May, 1865, to May, 1866. By Whitlaw Reid, Librarian to the House of Representatives. Illustrated. Post 8vo. price 10s. 6d.

Thirty Years of Army Life on the Border; Comprising Descriptions of the Indian Nomads of the Plains, Explorations of New Territory, a Trip across the Rocky Mountains in the Winter; Descriptions of the Habits of different Animals found in the West, and the Methods of Hunting them; with Incidents in the Lives of different Frontier Men, &c. By Colonel R. B. Marcy, U.S.A., Author of " The Prairie Traveller." With numerous Illustrations. 8vo. price 12s.

INDIA, AMERICA, AND THE COLONIES.

HISTORY of the Discovery and Exploration of Australia; or an Account of the Progress of Geographical Discovery in that Continent, from the Earliest Period to the Present Day. By the Rev. Julian E. Tenison Woods, F.R.G.S., &c., &c. 2 vols. demy 8vo. cloth, 28s.

South Australia : its Progress and Prosperity. By A. Forster, Esq. Demy 8vo. cloth, with Map, 15s.

Canada in 1864; a Hand-book for Settlers. By Henry T. N. Chesshyre. Fcap. 8vo. 2s. 6d.

" *When a man has something to say he can convey a good deal of matter in a few words. This book is but a small book, yet it leaves nothing untold that requires telling. The author is himself a settler, and knows what information is most necessary for those who are about to become settlers.*" —Athenæum.

Jamaica and the Colonial Office : Who caused the Crisis ? By George Price, Esq. late Member of the Executive Committees of Governors. 8vo. cloth, with a Plan, 5s.

The Colony of Victoria : its History, Commerce, and Gold Mining: its Social and Political Institutions, down to the End of 1863. With Remarks, Incidental and Comparative, upon the other Australian Colonies. By William Westgarth, Author of " Victoria and the Gold Mines," &c. 8vo. with a Map, cloth, 16s.

Tracks of McKinlay and Party across Australia. By John Davis, one of the Expedition. With an Introductory View of recent Explorations. By Wm. Westgarth. With numerous Illustrations in chromolithography, and Map. 8vo. cloth, 16s.

The Progress and Present State of British India; a Manual of Indian History, Geography, and Finance, for general use; based upon Official Documents, furnished under the authority of Her Majesty's Secretary of State for India. By Montgomery Martin, Esq., Author of a " History of the British Colonies," &c. Post 8vo. cloth, 10s. 6d.

The Cotton Kingdom : a Traveller's Observations on Cotton and Slavery in America, based upon three former volumes of Travels and Explorations. By Frederick Law Olmsted. With Map. 2 vols. post 8vo. 1l. 1s.

A History of the Origin, Formation, and Adoption of the Constitution of the United States of America, with Notices of its Principal Framers. By George Ticknor Curtis, Esq. 2 vols. 8vo. Cloth, 1l. 4s.

The Principles of Political Economy applied to the Condition, the Resources, and Institutions of the American People. By Francis Bowen. 8vo. Cloth, 14s.

A History of New South Wales from the Discovery of New Holland in 1616 to the present time. By the late Roderick Flanagan, Esq., Member of the Philosophical Society of New South Wales. 2 vols. 8vo. 24s.

Canada and its Resources. Two Prize Essays, by Hogan and Morris. 7s., or separately, 1s. 6d. each, and Map, 3s.

SCIENCE AND DISCOVERY.

DICTIONARY of Photography, on the Basis of Sutton's Dictionary. Rewritten by Professor Dawson, of King's College, Editor of the "Journal of Photography;" and Thomas Sutton, B.A., Editor of "Photograph Notes." 8vo. with numerous Illustrations.

A History of the Atlantic Telegraph. By Henry M. Field. 12mo. 7s. 6d.

The Physical Geography of the Sea and its Meteorology; or, the Economy of the Sea and its Adaptations, its Salts, its Waters, its Climates, its Inhabitants, and whatever there may be of general interest in its Commercial Uses or Industrial Pursuits. By Commander M. F. Maury, LL.D. Tenth Edition. With Charts. Post 8vo. cloth extra, 5s.

" *To Capt in Maury we are indebted for much information—indeed, for all that man kind possesses—of the crust of the earth beneath the blue waters of the Atlantic and Pacific oceans. Hopelessly scientific would these subjects be in the hands of most men, yet upon each and all of them Captain Maury enlists our attention, or charms us with explanations and theories, replete with originality and genius. His is indeed a nautical manual, a hand-book of the sea, investing with fresh interest every wave that beats upon our shores; and it cannot fail to awaken in both sailors and landsmen a craving to know more intimately the secrets of that wonderful element. The good that Maury has done in awakening the powers of observation of the Royal and Mercantile Navies of England and America is incalculable.*"—Blackwood's Magazine.

The Structure of Animal Life. By Louis Agassiz. With 46 Diagrams. 8vo. cloth, 10s. 6d.

The Kedge Anchor; or, Young Sailor's Assistant, by William Brady. Seventy Illustrations. 8vo. 16s.

Theory of the Winds, by Capt. Charles Wilkes. 8vo. cl. 8s. 6d.

Archaia; or, Studies of the Cosmogony and Natural History of the Hebrew Scriptures. By Professor Dawson, Principal of McGill College, Canada. Post 8vo. cloth, cheaper edition, 6s.

Ichnographs, from the Sandstone of the Connecticut River, Massachusetts, U.S.A. By James Dean, M.D. One volume, 4to. with Forty-six Plates. cloth, 27s.

The Recent Progress of Astronomy, by Elias Loomis, LL.D. 3rd Edition. Post 8vo. 7s. 6d.

An Introduction to Practical Astronomy, by the Same. 8vo. cloth. 8s.

Manual of Mineralogy, including Observations on Mines, Rocks, Reduction of Ores, and the Application of the Science to the Arts, with 260 Illustrations. Designed for the Use of Schools and Colleges. By James D. Dana, A.M., Author of a "System of Mineralogy." New Edition, revised and enlarged. 12mo. Half bound, 7s. 6d.

Cyclopædia of Mathematical Science, by Davies and Peck. 8vo. Sheep. 18s.

TRADE, AGRICULTURE, DOMESTIC ECONOMY, ETC.

UNT'S Merchants' Magazine (Monthly). 2s. 6d.

The Book of Farm Implements, and their Construction; by John L. Thomas. With 200 Illustrations. 12mo. 6s. 6d.

The Practical Surveyor's Guide; by A. Duncan. Fcp. 8vo. 4s. 6d.

Villas and Cottages; by Calvert Vaux, Architect. 300 Illustrations. 8vo. cloth. 12s.

Bee-Keeping. By "The Times" Bee-master. Small post 8vo. numerous Illustrations, cloth, 5s.

The English and Australian Cookery Book. Small post 8vo. Coloured Illustrations, cloth extra, 4s. 6d.

The Bubbles of Finance : the Revelations of a City Man. Fcap. 8vo. fancy boards, price 2s. 6d.

Coffee : A Treatise on its Nature and Cultivation. With some remarks on the management and purchase of Coffee Estates. By Arthur R. W. Lascelles. Post 8vo. cloth, 2s. 6d.

The Railway Freighter's Guide. Defining mutual liabilities of Carriers and Freighters, and explaining system of rates, accounts, invoices, checks, booking, and permits, and all other details pertaining to traffic management, as sanctioned by Acts of Parliament, Bye-laws, and General Usage. By J. S. Martin. 12mo. Cloth, 2s. 6d.

THEOLOGY.

HE VICARIOUS SACRIFICE; grounded on Principles of Universal Obligation. By Horace Bushnell, D.D. Author of "Nature and the Supernatural, &c. Crown 8vo. price 7s. 6d.

"*An important contribution to theological literature, whether we regard the amount of thought which it contains, the systematic nature of the treatise, or the practical effect of its teaching. . . . No one can rise from the study of his book without having his mind enlarged by its profound speculation, his devotion stirred by its piety, and his faith established on a broader basis of thought and knowledge.*"—Guardian.

Also by the same Author.
Christ and His Salvation. 6s.
Nature and the Supernatural. 3s. 6d.
Christian Nurture. 1s. 6d.
Character of Jesus. 6d.
New Life. 1s. 6d.
Work and Play. 3s. 6d.

The Land and the Book, or Biblical Illustrations drawn from the Manners and Customs, the Scenes and the Scenery of the Holy Land, by W. M. Thomson, M.D., twenty-five years a Missionary in Syria and Palestine. With 3 Maps and several hundred Illustrations. 2 vols. Post 8vo. cloth. 1l. 1s.

Missionary Geography for the use of Teachers and Missionary Collectors. Fcap. 8vo. with numerous maps and illustrations, 3s. 6d.

A Topographical Picture of Ancient Jerusalem ; beautifully coloured. Nine feet by six feet, on rollers, varnished. 3l. 3s.

The Light of the World: a most True Relation of a Pilgrimess travelling towards Eternity. Divided into Three Parts; which deserve to be read, understood, and considered by all who desire to be saved. Reprinted from the edition of 1696. Beautifully printed by Clay on toned paper. Crown 8vo. pp. 593, bevelled boards, 10s. 6d.

The Mission of Great Sufferings. By Elihu Burritt. Crown 8vo.

Faith's Work Perfected. The Rise and Progress of the Orphan Houses of Halle. From the German of Francke. By William L. Gage. Fcap.

The Life of the late Dr. Mountain, Bishop of Quebec. 8vo. cloth, price 10s. 6d.

A Short Method of Prayer; an Analysis of a Work so entitled by Madame de la Mothe-Guyon; by Thomas C. Upham, Professor of Mental and Moral Philosophy in Bowdoin College, U.S. America. Printed by Whittingham. 12mo. cloth. 1s.

Christian Believing and Living. By F. D. Huntington, D.D. Crown 8vo. cloth, 3s. 6d.

Life Thoughts. By the Rev. Henry Ward Beecher. Two Series, complete in one volume, well printed and well bound. 2s. 6d. Superior edition, illustrated with ornamental borders. Sm. 4to. cloth extra. 7s. 6d.

Dr. Beecher's Life and Correspondence: an Autobiography. Edited by his Son. 2 vols. post 8vo. with Illustrations, price 21s.

Life and Experience of Madame de la Mothe Guyon. By Professor Upham. Edited by an English Clergyman. Crown 8vo. cloth, with Portrait. Third Edition, 7s. 6d.

By the same Author.

Life of Madame Catherine Adorna; 12mo. cloth. 4s. 6d.
The Life of Faith, and Interior Life. 2 vols. 5s. 6d. each.
The Divine Union. 7s. 6d.

LAW AND JURISPRUDENCE.

HEATON'S Elements of International Law. An entirely new edition, edited by R. F. Dana, Author of "Two Years before the Mast," &c. Royal 8vo. cloth extra, 30s.

History of the Law of Nations; by Henry Wheaton. LL.D. author of the " Elements of International Law." Roy. 8vo. cloth, 31s. 6d.

Commentaries on American Law; by Chancellor Kent. Ninth and entirely New Edition. 4 vols. 8vo. calf. 5l. 5s.; cloth, 4l. 10s.

Treatise on the Law of Evidence; by Simon Greenleaf, LL.D. 3 vols. 8vo. calf. 4l. 4s.

Treatise on the Measure of Damages; or, An Enquiry into the Principles which govern the Amount of Compensation in Courts of Justice. By Theodore Sedgwick. Third revised Edition, enlarged. Imperial 8vo. cloth. 31s. 6d.

Justice Story's Commentaries on the Constitution of the United States. 2 vols. 36s.

Justice Story's Commentaries on the Laws, viz. Bailments—
Agency—Bills of Exchange—Promissory Notes—Partnership—and Conflict of Laws. 6 vols. 8vo. cloth, each 28s.

Justice Story's Equity Jurisprudence. 2 vols. 8vo. 63s.; and
Equity Pleadings. 1 vol. 8vo. 31s. 6d.

W. W. Story's Treatise on the Law of Contracts. Fourth Edition, greatly enlarged and revised. 2 vols. 8vo. cloth, 63s.

MEDICAL.

UMAN Physiology, Statical and Dynamical; by Dr.
Draper. 300 Illustrations. 8vo. 25s.

A Treatise on the Practice of Medicine; by Dr. George
B. Wood. Fourth Edition. 2 vols. 36s.

A Treatise on Fractures, by J. F. Malgaigne, Chirurgien de
l'Hôpital Saint Louis, Translated, with Notes and Additions, by John H.
Packard, M.D. With 106 Illustrations. 8vo. sheep. 1l. 1s.

The History of Prostitution; its Extent, Causes, and Effects
throughout the World: by William Sanger, M.D. 8vo. cloth. 16s.

Elements of Chemical Physics; with numerous Illustrations.
By Josiah P. Cooke. 8vo. cloth. 16s.
" As an introduction to Chemical Physics, this is by far the most com-
prehensive work in our language."—Athenæum, Nov. 17.

A History of Medicine, from its Origin to the Nineteenth Century.
By Dr. P. V. Renouard. 8vo. 18s.

Letters to a Young Physician just entering upon Practice; by
James Jackson, M.D. Fcp. 8vo. 5s.

Lectures on the Diseases of Women and Children. By Dr. G. S.
Bedford. 4th Edition. 8vo. 18s.

The Principles and Practice of Obstetrics. By Gunning S.
Bedford, A.M., M.D. With Engravings. 8vo. Cloth, 1l. 1s.

Principles and Practice of Dental Surgery; by C. A. Harris. 6th
Edition. 8vo. 24s.

Chemical and Pharmaceutical Manipulations; by C. and C. Morfit.
Royal 8vo. Second Edition enlarged. 21s.

FICTION AND MISCELLANEOUS.

OILERS of the Sea. By Victor Hugo. Translated by
W. Moy Thomas. 3 vols. crown 8vo, 24s.
Cheap edit. With a Frontispiece by Gustave Doré. Cr. 8vo. 6s.

A Casual Acquaintance. By Mrs. Duffus Hardy.
2 vols. post 8vo, 16s.

The Story of Kennett. By Bayard Taylor. 2 vols. post 8vo, 16s.

Mr. Charles Reade's celebrated Romance, Hard Cash. A new
and cheap Standard Edition. Price 6s. handsomely bound in cloth.

Passing the Time. By Blanchard Jerrold. 2 vols. post 8vo. 16s.

Marian Rooke. By Henry Sedley. 3 vols. 24s.

The Gayworthys. 3rd edition, 3s. 6d. crown 8vo. 1s. 6d. boards.

Sir Felix Foy, Bart. By Dutton Cook. 3 vols. post 8vo. 24s.
The Trials of the Tredgolds. By the same. 3 vols. 24s.

A Mere Story. By the Author of "Twice Lost." 3 vols. 24s.

Selvaggio. By the Author of "Mary Powell." One vol. 8s.

Miss Biddy Frobisher. By the Author of "Selvaggio. One vol.
8s.

John Godfrey's Fortunes. By Bayard Taylor. 3 vols. 24s.
Hannah Thurston. By the same Author. 3 vols. 24s.

A Splendid Fortune. By J. Hain Friswell. 3 vols. post 8vo. 24s.

Lion-Hearted; a Novel. By Mrs. Grey. 2 vols. post 8vo. 16s.

A Dangerous Secret. By Annie Thomas. 2 vols. 16s.

Lynn of the Craggs. By Charlotte Smith. 3 vols. post 8vo. 24s.

Unconventional. By Thomas Sutton. 3 vols. post 8vo, 24s.

St. Agnes Bay; or, Love at First Sight. Post 8vo. cloth, 7s.

The White Favour. By H. Holl. 3 vols. 24s.

The Old House in Crosby Square. By Henry Holl. 2 vols. 16s.
More Secrets than One. By the same Author. 3 vols. 24s.

Strathcairn. By Charles Allston Collins. 2 vols. post 8vo. 16s.

A Good Fight in the Battle of Life : a Prize Story founded on
Facts. Reprinted by permission from "Cassell's Family Paper."
Crown 8vo. cloth, 7s. 6d.

Female Life in Prison. By a Prison Matron. Fourth and
cheaper edition : with a Photograph, by permission, from the engraving
of Mrs. Fry reading to the Prisoners in 1816. 1 vol. crown 8vo., 5s.

Myself and My Relatives. *Second Thousand.* With Frontispiece on Steel from a Drawing by John E. Millais, A.R.A. Cr. 8vo. 5s.

Tales for the Marines. By Walter Thornbury. 2 vols. post
8vo. 16s.
"*Who would not wish to be a Marine, if that would secure a succession
of tales like these?*"—Athenæum.

Helen Felton's Question : a Book for Girls By Agnes Wylde.
Cheaper Edition, with Frontispiece. Crown 8vo. 3s. 6d.

Faith Gartney's Girlhood. By the Author of "The Gayworthys." Fcap. 8vo. with coloured Frontispiece, cloth, price 3s. 6d.;
or, Railway Edition, boards, 1s. 6d.

The Professor at the Breakfast Table. By Oliver W. Holmes,
Author of the "Autocrat of the Breakfast Table." Fcap. 3s. 6d.

The Rooks' Garden, and other Papers. By Cuthbert Bede,
Author of "The Adventures of Mr. Verdant Green." Choicely printed
by Constable. Post 8vo. 7s. 6d.

Hobson's Choice. A Story by Dutton Cook. Reprinted from " Once a Week." Post 8vo.

The Masque at Ludlow, and other Romanesques. By the Author of " Mary Powell." Post 8vo.

A Summer in Leslie Goldthwaite's Life. By the Author of " The Gayworthys." With Illustrations. Fcap. 8vo.

The Chimney Corner. By Mrs. H. B. Stowe. Uniform with " The Little Foxes." Cheap and Library Editions.

The Journal of a Waiting Gentlewoman. Edited by Beatrice A. Jourdan. Post 8vo. 8s.

The White Wife; with other stories, Supernatural, Romantic and Legendary. Collected and Illustrated by Cuthbert Bede. Post 8vo. cloth, 6s.

Wayside Warbles. By Edward Capern, Rural Postman, Bideford, Devon. Fcap. 8vo. cloth, 5s.

Last Gleanings. By the late Frank Fowler. Post 8vo. cloth, 7s. 6d.

House and Home Papers. By Mrs. H. B. Stowe. 12mo. boards, 1s.; cloth extra, 2s. 6d.

Little Foxes. By Mrs. H. B. Stowe. Cloth extra, 3s. 6d. Popular Edition, fancy boards, 1s.

The Pearl of Orr's Island. A Story of the Coast of Maine. By Mrs. Harriet Beecher Stowe. Author of " Uncle Tom's Cabin." " Minister's Wooing." In popular form, Part I. 1s. 6d.; Part II. 2s.; or, complete in one volume, with engraving on steel from water-colour by John Gilbert. Handsomely bound in cloth, 5s.

The Minister's Wooing: a Tale of New England. By the Author of " Uncle Tom's Cabin." Two Editions :—1. In post 8vo. cloth, with Thirteen Illustrations by Hablot K. Browne. 5s.—2. Popular Edition, crown 8vo. cloth, with a Design by the same Artist. 2s. 6d.

Nothing to Wear, and Two Millions, by William Allen Butler. 1s.

Railway Editions of Popular Fiction. On good paper, well-printed and bound, fancy boards.

Paul Foster's Daughter. 2s. 6d.

The Lost Sir Massingberd. 2s. 6d.

The Bubbles of Finance. 2s. 6d.

Profits of Panics. 1s.

The Gayworthys. 1s. 6d.

The Autocrat of the Breakfast Table. 1s.

The King's Mail. 2s. 6d.

Faith Gartney's Girlhood. 1s. 6d.

My Lady Ludlow. 2s. 6d.

Mrs. Stowe's Little Foxes. 1s.

———— House and Home. 1s.

Chimney Corner. 1s.

Abel Drake's Wife, 2s. 6d.

Footsteps Behind Him, 2s. 6d.

When the Snow Falls, 2s. 6d.

LONDON: SAMPSON LOW, SON, AND MARSTON.
MILTON HOUSE, LUDGATE HILL.

English, American, and Colonial Booksellers and Publishers.

Chiswick Press :—Whittingham and Wilkins, Tooks Court, Chancery Lane.